karmic
astroLogy

ABOUT THE AUTHOR

Ruth Aharoni (Israel) is a professional astrologer and certified yoga teacher, with over twenty-five years of experience in both fields. She holds a B.A. in literature and philosophy, and is also a certified Life Coach and NLP practitioner. She is the author of several books on yoga, astrology, channeling, tarot, and children's books for body and soul, and conducts workshops on spiritual growth and self-empowerment.

TO WRITE TO THE AUTHOR

If you wish to contact the author or would like more information about this book, please write to the author in care of Llewellyn Worldwide and we will forward your request. Both the author and publisher appreciate hearing from you and learning of your enjoyment of this book and how it has helped you. Llewellyn Worldwide cannot guarantee that every letter written to the author can be answered, but all will be forwarded. Please write to:

Ruth Aharoni
℅ Llewellyn Worldwide
2143 Wooddale Drive, Dept. 978-0-7387-0967-3
Woodbury, Minnesota 55125-2989, U.S.A.

Please enclose a self-addressed stamped envelope for reply,
or $1.00 to cover costs. If outside U.S.A., enclose
international postal reply coupon.
Many of Llewellyn's authors have websites with additional information and resources.
For more information, please visit our website at http://www.llewellyn.com

RUTH AHARONI

karmic astroLogy

PAST LIVES, PRESENT LOVES

Llewellyn Publications
Woodbury, Minnesota

First Edition
Second Printing, 2007

Originally published in 1999 by Or'Am Publishing House, Tel Aviv, Israel, under the title *The Karmic Connection*.
Hebrew copyright © 1999 Or'Am Publishing House.
Many thanks to the translator, Miriam Erez, who rendered the Hebrew into English.

Cover art (planets) © PhotoDisc
Cover design by Ellen Dahl
Llewellyn is a registered trademark of Llewellyn Worldwide, Ltd.

The Edgar Cayce readings in chapter 11 are © 1971, 1993, 2004 by the Edgar Cayce Foundation and are used by permission.

Library of Congress Cataloging-in-Publication Data for *Karmic Astrology* is on file at the Library of Congress.
ISBN 13: 978-0-7387-0967-3
ISBN 10: 0-7387-0967-0

Llewellyn Publications
A Division of Llewellyn Worldwide, Ltd.
2143 Wooddale Drive, Dept. 978-0-7387-0967-3
Woodbury, Minnesota 55125-2989, U.S.A.
www.llewellyn.com

Printed in the United States of America

OTHER BOOKS BY RUTH AHARONI

In Hebrew:

Somebody Please Open a Window
(Neorah Press, 2007)

Yoga for Me and You and the Children Too (4th Edition)
(Neorah Press, 2005)

Channeling in Ten Lessons
(Neorah Press, 2004)

The Karmic Connection: Reincarnation, Relationships and Astrology (2nd Edition)
(Or'Am Publishing House, 2004)

Cups or Swords: Improving Your Love Life with the Tarot
(Or'Am Publishing House, 2001)

Heaven Can Answer: Horary Astrology
(Notzah va'Keset, 1993)

Dedicated to all the souls
Who search diligently
For the Truth

CONTENTS

FIGURES

A WORD ON RETURNING
TO THE PAST

Of time you would make a stream upon whose bank you would sit and watch its flowing.
Yet the timeless in you is aware of life's timelessness,
And knows that yesterday is but today's memory and tomorrow is today's dream.
And that that which sings and contemplates in you is still dwelling
within the bounds of that first moment which scattered the stars into space.

—"THE TIME" FROM *The Prophet* BY KAHLIL GIBRAN

W hen I was ten, I came down with an ordinary case of the winter flu. It wasn't the first time I'd been sick—I had graduated with honors from all of the usual childhood diseases. In fact, every winter I eagerly awaited the first signs of illness. What schoolchild doesn't want an unofficial vacation once in a while? In my case, such sick holidays included the added advantage of being pampered by a nurturing mother whose Moon sign is Virgo. This time I curled up under the blankets, stacks of books and games surrounding me, as befits a Sagittarius, ready to spend a pleasant few days in bed.

Suddenly—and I remember the suddenness of it—a deathly fear seized me. I was certain that I was about to die. I called for my mother, and she sat beside me and with endless patience explained to me that I was not in danger of dying and that I'd soon be well. It took her a while to convince me. The fear had gripped my heart and wouldn't let go. Of course, a few days later, I was indeed well again. A few years later, I internalized the concept of reincarnation, and that deathly fear never visited me again.

I forgot the incident for many years. Then one day, as I was meditating, I found myself in another existence in which I was a ten-year-old girl in Italy. I lay in bed, deathly ill with pneumonia, and experienced my death from the illness. Only two days after this meditation did the memory of the incident from my childhood come back to me, and with it the explanation of the panic that had so suddenly gripped me. Since then, I have experienced my death in several other incarnations. In some cases the circumstances were traumatic, and in others death came as a liberating experience.

Reliving past lives by means of the regression technique is one of the skills that I have acquired in the process of my spiritual search. Through regression, I have experienced many incarnations stretching across entire time periods, continents, and cultures. The return to past lives that can explain present personal issues is fascinating; I have returned to past lives in which I engaged in yoga, astrology, spiritual healing, and reading Tarot cards.

I've been a monk in both India and Tibet, a member of the Essene sect in the Judaean Desert, and a nun in Poland. I was surprised to discover that in the fourteenth century I was trained in astrology in a convent in France. Up until that particular regression, I had believed that the Church opposed astrology. This discovery motivated me to research the subject, and I learned that many members of the clergy, even high-ranking curates, engaged in astrology.

For years in my present life I avoided Tarot cards, until their magical attraction overcame my resistance. I began to read them and even to impart this art to others. In one of my travels into my past, I discovered that in the eighteenth century my skill and proficiency at Tarot reading had led to my forced servitude to people who exploited my talents. This traumatic experience, which was imprinted on my subconscious, explained my initial reluctance to engage in Tarot reading in this life.

I experienced other existences, some of which took place thousands of years ago. Every return to the past explained and clarified more patterns and phenomena in my present life.

Returning to past lives is not a gimmick to be used to satisfy one's curiosity or flatter one's ego. Every link to past lives adds to our storehouse of knowledge about ourselves, our surroundings, and the path of our present lives, helping us identify our goals and destinies. In addition, in some cases we suffer from physical ailments, distress, or fears whose origins cannot be found in the events or circumstances of our present lives, but rather can be traced to other incarnations. Discovering these origins can liberate us from their negative effects.

The origins of couples' relationships also usually lie in past incarnations, and because relationships are the most common issue among those coming for consultations, what appealed to me most regarding reincarnation was the study of *karmic connections*.

In my practice, I've met couples who were perfectly matched in every respect, yet whose life circumstances prevented them from being together; couples who couldn't live with each other, yet couldn't live without each other either; and couples who joined forces for a shared cause and then, having completed their mutual karmic work, went their separate ways. I've studied the birth charts of both married and unmarried couples and of parent-child, sibling, teacher-pupil, and friend pairs. Each chart comparison was interesting to me, if not personally, then professionally.

I've developed a particular interest in the karmic connection of Edgar Cayce, the "Sleeping Prophet" about whose life and beliefs many books have been written. Cayce was happily married to Gertrude, yet in his spiritual readings, which he performed while in a trance, he indicated that his secretary, Gladys Davis, was actually his cosmic partner. I inquired at the Association for Research and Enlightenment (A.R.E.) in Virginia Beach, Virginia, requesting the birth data of Edgar, Gertrude, and Gladys, which I did receive. I then added their birth charts to my research and use them as examples throughout this book.

Throughout my research, I studied many factors in order to decide whether they were significant in chart comparison, and whether they contributed to understanding karmic connections between those represented by the charts. I studied the Part of Fortune and the Part of Marriage, the Antiscia, the Vertex and Anti-Vertex, the Moon's phases, the effect of Chiron on chart comparison, and other factors.

After completing a comprehensive study, however, I decided not to include the above information in this book. I chose to focus this book on factors that, based on my conclusions, provide the basic information required for understanding karmic connections, which will also enable beginners in astrology to experience their first taste of chart comparison. Presented herein are the building blocks of astrology—the signs, planets, aspects, and houses—from the point of view of karmic astrology, with an emphasis on karmic relationships.

In chapters 5, 6, and 7, I walk the reader through a simple yet instructive chart comparison. Chapters 9 and 10 are dedicated to the nodal axis (the Dragon's Head and Tail), which plays a central role in karmic astrology. The appendix gives the locations of the nodes in signs starting at the beginning of the twentieth century, enabling you to obtain clues to your life's karmic path. Chapter 11, "Karmic Couples and Cosmic Couples," contains material based on the findings of my research.

The analysis of a birth chart from a karmic point of view does not indicate specific incarnations, but rather shows energy patterns imprinted on a person throughout his or her incarnations and whose influence is apparent in the person's present life, dictating certain choices made. In order to identify specific incarnations, I use channeling. An example of a birth chart from a former life derived from a regression and channeling session appears in chapter 11.

The final chapter, "Spiritual Attraction," deals with developing awareness, self-improvement, and the possibility of finding a cosmic partner through work on the *chakras*, or the system of energy centers located in the etheric body. This chapter presents in detail each chakra and its role in our physical, mental, and spiritual lives. Chakra work has great significance in the New Age, and this chapter offers simple yet effective exercises that aid in the development of all areas of life. I recommend that you incorporate these exercises into your everyday routine.

A note on semantics: Throughout this book, I use the term "the incarnating soul" to mean the renewed embodiment of a soul inside a body in the present life. This term relates to the story of Adam and Eve in the Garden of Eden. According to Kabbalistic interpretation, Adam and Eve lived in the Garden as souls without a physical embodiment. The act of eating the fruit of the Tree of Knowledge expressed the human desire to experience existence on an earthly, physical level.

Existence in the physical world entails sadness, suffering, pain, and death. God warns Adam and Eve against eating the fruit of the Tree of Knowledge "lest you shall die," and after they eat of it, God decrees: "By the sweat of thy face shalt thou eat bread, till thou return unto the ground; for out of it wast thou taken; for dust thou art, and unto dust shalt thou return."—Genesis 3:19.

Genesis 3:21 tells how God "made for Adam and for his wife garments of skins, and clothed them." The mystical meaning of this verse is that in order to survive on Earth, humans must "grow skin," or assume a physical, or carnal, form, therefore *incarnating*. The root of the Hebrew word *karam*, which means "grew skin," is the same as that of the word *karma*; i.e., karma is accumulated only in the physical world. We can pay our karmic debt only through life on this Earth—in our carnal form—as our "incarnating soul" chooses the proper conditions for fulfilling its karma.

CHAPTER ONE

KARMA, INCARNATIONS, AND THE BIRTH CHART

Upon bursting forth from the womb
The passing moment was imprinted
By the celestial seal
And the universal soul inspired in you
The touch of immortality.

—RUTH AHARONI

The word karma has by now earned itself a respected place in our language, having been accepted into the modern-day lexicon. In popular use, karma means "fate," yet this usage is simplistic and compromises the dignity of the original meaning.

The literal meaning of karma in Sanskrit, the ancient Indian language from which it came, is "action" or "act"; that is to say that any action—physical or mental—is karma. Deeds are physical karma, and thoughts, emotions, desire, imagination, and will are mental karma. Mental action precedes physical action, or actually creates it; that is, every deed or act is preceded by an initial thought.

Yet karma is not only action; it is also the result of every action, because the result is actually an integral part of the action. Every phenomenon has a cause. The spinning and the spinner—or the cause and the result—are intertwined, and herein originates the law of karma, which is actually the law of causality.

The world is driven by the law of karma, which is a natural law to which all other natural laws are subordinate. The law of inertia, the law of cause and effect, and the law of reward and retribution are all contained within the larger law of causality.

Exodus 21:22 expresses the law of reward and retribution blatantly: "An eye for an eye, a tooth for a tooth," meaning that whoever harms will be harmed, no matter when, where, or by whom. Good deeds bring reward, and bad deeds bring punishment. An eye for an eye means that for every action, there must be a response, which will always be identical in degree and similar in kind. What we did for someone or harm that we caused someone in a former life will come back to us in this life or a life to come, just as a boomerang returns to its thrower. The deeper meaning of this concept is that certain difficulties that we experience have their origins in our soul's readiness to experience in this life injustices that we inflicted upon others in past lives, in order for us to learn from this.

At the foundation of the law of karma lies the belief that life is an ongoing experience that is not limited to one incarnation. In order to find the cause of a certain event that happened to us, it is not enough to look in the present life; we must also examine previous lives. Life does not end with the death of the body; the soul is eternal and continues to live. What happens to us in the present may be the consequence of something that happened in the near or ancient past. Our mental, physical, familial, and economic conditions are all the consequences of all of our past lives, of our accumulated karma.

This world has no chaos or caprice; things don't happen by coincidence. There is a logical sequence of actions and consequences, with a connection between what we have done in the past and what will happen to us in the future. It's not a matter of payback or punishment handed down from above. It's not that injustice or discrimination are being manipulated by some transcendental force, making one or the other of us rich or poor, happy or miserable.

Each of us is responsible for our own deeds, and as such, for the results of those deeds; herein lies justice in its purest form. When our vision is limited, we fail to understand this law, so that we define what happens to us as simply "our fate." Yet if we understand that our present life is only the blink of an eye in relation to the entire life of our soul, then we can understand that there is a karmic scale upon which everything is measured and weighed.

The universal law of karma operates everywhere, all the time, without a break, and with scientific precision. It operates on both the physical and the mental level, and it is actually a means of achieving universal justice and cosmic balance. It is a law that places every one of us in situations that enable lessons to be learned—lessons necessary for our spiritual development.

Karma can be divided into three categories:

Sanchita: This term refers to the reservoir of karma—good or bad—that we have accumulated over many incarnations. In each incarnation, only some of this reservoir is activated, as activation of all of it would overwhelm us both physically and mentally. Part of this karmic backlog is embodied in the character of the individual, in his or her qualities, tendencies, talents, aspirations, and desires.

Prarabdha: This is considered fate, or the karma that we must withstand in this life. There is no escaping prarabdha, and it is unchangeable. Prarabdha is the part of karma that is incumbent upon each individual to complete or to balance in this life. This karma is determined prior to birth by a person's soul; the chosen karma must happen, and is experienced by the person as fate.

Kriyamana: This is the karma that we create in this life, and we deal with its consequences later. This karma goes into our overall "karmic bank account," or sanchita. Our objective in this life should be to create good karma and endeavor to avoid creating bad karma. If we "collect points" for good deeds, then we can add them to our positive balance, whose fruits we can enjoy in the future. If we "use up our credit," then we'll be in karmic debt, which we'll have to cover in the future. Each of us has freedom of choice and free will at any given moment, and these determine our deeds; today's deed-karma becomes tomorrow's fate-karma.

As long as we reincarnate, we are subordinate to the law of karma. The karmic patterns with which we must cope can help us grapple with our fate with understanding, patience, and reinforced energy.

Each of us must be born again and again until we reach self-knowledge, or the true and eternal self, which is the godhood in each of us. Our souls contain all of the potential godly energies, and the reason for the soul's entry into the physical world is to provide the experiences necessary to activate these energies and transform them from the potential to the actual. The repeating physical embodiment of the soul happens, among other reasons, so that spiritual lessons such as love, compassion, tolerance, moderation, balance, humility, purity of heart, giving, and devotion can be learned.

The imprints of everything that an individual has ever experienced are absorbed and stored in the consciousness. The consciousness does not need the body, and does not wear out with the perishing of the body that the soul "wears" in each incarnation. These imprints are activated throughout the incarnations, and the end of the cycle of incarnations is anticipated only when the soul has evolved—when it has experienced and learned enough in the physical world, and no longer has the will to be reborn, which is the force that drives it to come back and assume a physical form.

It is incumbent upon the soul to reach a level of consciousness that goes beyond the dictates of either karma or illusion, both of which are created in the world of three dimensions. The fundamental objective of reincarnation is the soul's improvement and evolution, and the number of times that a person must return and be born depends upon the degree of improvement that the soul takes upon itself in each incarnation.

One of the main motivators for a soul to begin anew is its need to experience freedom of choice. The soul needs a physical body, because only in the physical world does it occupy a position of choice, which it did not have when it was a part of the pure cosmic consciousness.

According to the Kabbalah, the Jewish mystical writings, the task on behalf of which the soul departs from the soul of the Creation is its will to achieve the good of the Creator out of merit, not out of charity; as such, it is "poised at the starting line" of the path of incarnations to begin the "race." Its goal is the capacity for giving, and it will reach the finish line when it has learned to give only in tandem with the body, which, in Kabbalistic terms, contains within it "the will to receive for its own sake." Only then can the soul create completeness, or "the will to receive in order to give." When this task has been achieved, the soul no longer has need of physical embodiment.

In the breaks between lives, we have a broader vision than we do during our sojourn on Earth, and we process our understanding of all of our earthly experiences. This knowledge helps us choose and plan what we will experience the next time around.

The dilemma of "all is foreseen, yet freedom of choice is given" is solved when we accept reincarnation. Before each incarnation, we decide, aided by the cosmic forces, what objectives we want to fulfill, what lessons we still need to learn, and which path will balance our karma. Karma, even when manifested as a difficult fate, is the result of our soul's freedom of choice and free will. Karma is revealed when the time is right in order to give us an opportunity to balance and to repair.

When we try with all our being to change events or situations in our lives, but do not succeed in doing so, it is a sign that such events were planned in advance by our soul so that it could experience them. We have agreed in advance to rise to the task or challenge. Bereavement, illness, accidents, loss of property, and other painful events have their source in "repair work" that was planned in advance, whose purpose is to create an opportunity for spiritual growth and progress. The birth experience causes us to forget these choices, but understanding the meaning of suffering enables us to draw from these pre-made choices as a source of strength and an impetus for personal development.

The way we react to situations and events also depends on freedom of choice. Responses such as anger, grudges, self-pity, fear, regret, self-blame, blaming others, and so forth cause energy blockages and a renewal of negative karma. When we repair negative emotions from the past, we repair the events that gave rise to them, bringing closure, and thus helping to balance the karma. A spiritual approach and understanding and positive thoughts help us overcome negative karma, and we can accelerate the process of completing our karma by living a pure life.

Diligent souls that wish to "close their karmic account" as quickly as possible can decide before birth to take on many difficult experiences, as "suffering purges one's sins" (Talmud, tractate *Brachot* 7b). Thus we can settle in our minds the contradiction of "the righteous suffer, the wicked thrive" (Talmud, tractate *Brachot* 7a). Souls that have achieved a high spiritual level often take upon themselves the travails of Job, while souls that are less developed spiritually often choose a life in which the emphasis is on the material and the gratification of the body.

It is important to point out that even souls that have achieved a high spiritual level for several incarnations can experience setbacks in any given incarnation. In addition, occasionally, after several incarnations of hard work and a heavy yoke, or of extraordinary demonstrations of giving or leadership, a soul may decide to "take a break" and go for a simpler, easier life with few irregular events.

Freedom of choice enables the soul to choose a unique path that is right for it. Earthly existence is a training period; there are souls that choose a particular path over several incarnations in a row for the purpose of perfecting certain abilities or talents, while other souls choose to go for a range of experiences, throwing themselves into these varied experiences anew each time around.

The condition of one's karma at the time of one's death is what largely determines the soul's decisions for future incarnations. Our experiences form the right character for fulfilling *dharma*, or our correct direction in life, which in turn is determined by our goals.

Thoughts and aspirations from past lives can determine the characteristics in our present lives, and tendencies from the past can blossom into talents in the present. Good deeds done in the past give us "credit" for good life circumstances, and conversely, past bad deeds can be the cause for unhappiness in this life. All of our experiences from the past build our present consciousness.

Choice of a certain scenario of life requires being born in a particular planetary configuration; therefore, one is born at a time and a place that are compatible with his or her soul's karmic choice. So a birth chart, or horoscope, is actually a photograph of a soul's karma, showing the picture of all of a person's lives and revealing influences of the past and possibilities for the future.

A birth chart shows symbolically a person's basic life patterns, potential, qualities, talents, and problem areas. Through understanding the various factors in the chart, we can discover a person's energy patterns at all levels—physical, emotional, mental, and spiritual. The chart also reveals a person's past patterns, mental impressions gathered, and how this person is now a result of what he or she did and thought in past lives.

A person is actually the product of his or her consciousness throughout all of his or her incarnations, and the birth chart is therefore a map of that consciousness. The chart shows the limitations that a person sets for him- or herself in this existence, yet also the means available to him or her for progress and development. The use that a person makes of these means determines to what degree he or she will fulfill his or her potential, and this in turn depends upon freedom of choice.

One can overcome trials and get through challenges—symbolized in the chart by disharmonious planetary influences—and achieve whatever goals one has set for oneself, yet this can only be done with effort. A person with a powerful soul and spiritual energy will succeed. In this regard, the expression "The stars do not control our destiny" (Talmud, tractate *Shabbat*) is fitting, as it refers to an individual with an evolved soul who takes upon him- or herself spiritual discipline, leads a life of pure thoughts and ethics, and possesses high awareness and heightened cosmic knowledge. Such a person soars to great heights, releasing his or her soul from the bonds of the material world, so that the influences of the planets and signs do not affect him or her.

Humans were created in God's image, and what humans and God have in common is the capacity for Creation. The thoughts of the Creator brought about and still bring about the ongoing creation of the universe and our world. Humans too have the ability to create their world. Our thoughts create our reality. If we change the nature of our thoughts, then we can change ourselves, release ourselves from limitations, and expand the limits of our consciousness. If we avoid negative energy, apply our consciousness with perseverance to the highest energetic frequencies, and connect up to cosmic consciousness, then we can release ourselves from the bonds of karma and from the cycle of incarnations, and our soul can move through the infinite reality and express itself limitlessly.

chapter two

KARMIC ENCOUNTERS

Among the men and women, the multitude,
I perceive one picking me out by secret and divine signs,
Acknowledging none else—not parent, wife, husband, brother, child,
any nearer than I am;
Some are baffled—But that one is not—that one knows me.

Ah, lover and perfect equal!
I meant that you should discover me so, by my faint indirections;
And I, when I meet you, mean to discover you by the like in you.

—"Among the Multitude" from *Leaves of Grass* by Walt Whitman

Prior to a person's birth, the soul chooses the birth time and birthplace, enabling a planetary constellation that allows the realization of the soul's purpose in the present incarnation. One such purpose is "soul lessons" learned through renewed encounters with souls that we knew in past incarnations. *Karmic history* explains why upon meeting people, we feel an immediate pull toward certain people, or an immediate repulsion to others. If a certain relationship develops, it will reflect relationships from the past. Every present connection has a purpose that can be linked to past lives. This purpose could be a deepening of the connection, a balancing of negative karma between people, or the payoff of a debt, if there was any type of commitment between them. Occasionally the relationship happens in order to fulfill a combination of purposes.

When certain people enter our lives, even though we do not consciously remember meeting them in a past life, the soul remembers, and memories of the nature of the relationship, events, and experiences that we underwent with this person are stored in the subconscious. If previous relations with the person were negative, then this time they must be balanced and repaired through mutual positive action. If the previous relations were positive, then they will continue positively this time around, even improving, and we will enjoy the renewed relationship.

Only rarely do we find two people in a relationship who had no connection in the past, even if only briefly. Emotions from past lives continue from incarnation to incarnation, affecting our present lives. Problems in the relationship, even those resulting from present circumstances, are actually an outcome of unresolved problems from the past. Such problems continue to sprout and hover until we manage to solve them. Problematic relationships are actually learning opportunities, and if we are with a certain person today, it is because the right circumstances for shared karmic balance have been created.

Negative actions, thoughts, and behaviors create negative karma anew, which accumulates and will have to be treated in the future or in a future incarnation. When we react to relationships negatively—with bitterness, anger, guilt, vengeance, feelings of having been wronged, accusations, putdowns, and so forth—it is a sign that a past lesson was not learned, and at some point in the future, an opportunity will present itself to learn it, to rectify the situation, and to erase the negative karma.

This explains why relationships that seem implausible even happen at all. When we see a couple whose relationship looks untenable, it's clear as can be that the long arm of karma is involved. If the relationship goes unresolved, and the enmity is not brought to a close, then there is no doubt that the two people will have to meet again and again until their problems are solved and mutual harmony is achieved. However, understanding helps to overcome karma. Each one of us has something to learn from our present life, and our relationships are our "school" on the ascent to knowledge. If we learn the present lesson, then we can progress to the next lesson.

Lovers from the past are reborn again and again into a shared context, and each new encounter is intended as a lesson for the soul, and has been planned since before birth. Two people will be attracted even if neither remembers the past that they share, and love will happen anew. Many people have happy love relationships; their relationship with their partner was balanced in the past, and they met again in order to harvest the fruit of their love harmoniously.

Such partners have learned their relationship lessons of the past, and they are in the present relationship in order to develop in new realms. They have reaped their happiness through many traumatic experiences, both together and alone, in which they acquired wisdom and learned what true love is. In every new incarnation, their love for their partner will deepen, becoming less and less egoistical, until ultimately it is fused and complete.

People with whom we are close now were connected to us in another place in another time. Partners and lovers with whom we have developed emotional relationships and affinity in other incarnations are kindred souls, or *soulmates*. When we meet a soulmate, we feel an instant connection and closeness to that person. We feel comfortable with him or her, and may feel as if we've already met the person before, even if we're sure we have not.

Soulmates have shared past lives with us, although not necessarily in the same role that they fill in this life. However, it is likely that the person was our lover, friend, or relative in a past life. "Soulmate-hood" explains why out-of-the-ordinary relationships form between people who *seem*, from an outsider's viewpoint, to be very different from one another, such as two people of different nationalities or backgrounds, or between whom there is a wide age gap.

Soulmates also have various levels. There are soulmates that are *matched*, those that are *twins*, and those that *complete*. Astrologically, the various types can be identified by comparing two peoples' charts.

Between **matched souls** there is suitability, to one degree or another, that enables a pleasant friendship, common interests, strong family ties, good workplace relations, or living together harmoniously.

Occasionally we meet someone whose similarity to us is so compelling that we sense that the person is truly our **twin soul**. The twin soul can be either the same or the opposite gender, and sometimes can actually be a family member. The relationship may not always be easy, but there is a mutual emotional attraction and a high level of understanding. This understanding can sometimes be so strong that there is no need for words to communicate. We feel our twin soul's emotions and know his or her thoughts, and vice versa. We feel natural and open with a twin soul, and it may happen that periods of both our lives run parallel to each other. Yet even if the relationship doesn't continue as a lifelong one, the soul connection remains.

A special soulmate connection is that of **completing souls**. Each of us has only one completing soul, and the contact with that person creates a special energy field that exists only surrounding a pair of completing souls. Completing souls' energies are in such a state of synchrony that when they are together, their auras unite and create an "energy ball."

A completing soul is our ideal mate, but we may not meet this mate in every incarnation. If we do not meet our completing soul in this incarnation, it is likely that each of us has chosen to work on different lessons. And if we should meet our completing soul, for various reasons, it may not turn out that we live with the person; the relationship with one's completing soul is not necessarily harmonious from the beginning. Due to negative past karma, there may be problems in the relationship that must be resolved, yet there is an undercurrent of love that ultimately, sometime in the future, will triumph.

Even if we do not meet or live with our completing soul, we can form relationships with matching or twin souls, and build with them quite satisfying and supportive relationships.

A completing soul is our true partner, or our *cosmic partner*. A cosmic partnership is a special level of karmic relationship. While not every karmic partner is a cosmic partner, every cosmic partner is necessarily a karmic partner. Even if cosmic partners are not together in this life, they nevertheless "row" tirelessly toward their joining, and both work to "strengthen their breathing" at their own pace and as per their own ability.

According to various esoteric schools of thought, including the Kabbalah, true partners, male and female, are two halves of one soul that divided at the moment of the Creation, and each half was sent on its way, on a long journey in this world. After many incarnations, it is incumbent upon each half to achieve its restored state and to "balance its karmic debt."

The separating of the genders gives every entity an opportunity to "take the test of life" on Earth. The soul longs for its other half in order to complete its "route to restoration." Only thus can the soul return to its original, complete state.

Throughout the incarnations, each soul meets its true partner again and again. The partner is usually of the opposite gender, but occasionally, as a result of a desire to try a variety of experiences, a gender switch can take place, and both partners are born the same gender, which could be one explanation for homosexual relationships.

One's partner may take the form of a family member, a lover, or even an enemy whose "purpose" it is to cause suffering, which can be an intense means of accelerating spiritual development. Every relationship in every incarnation is a learning experience, and has the power to bring about repair, restoration, and a condition of heightened consciousness.

Some of us will learn true love only after many incarnations, while others will find their partners quickly. In the best scenario, both partners learn together, or at the same time. However, if it happens that only one partner learns his or her lesson, then the other will need to learn it, but with another partner. Occasionally we may actually learn what true couplehood is from someone who is not our true partner, but is nevertheless a good partner for us, and thus that person aids us in balancing the shared karma.

It does happen that true partners meet and live together, yet there are factors separating them that cause them to split up. It also happens that a person does not realize that he or she has come across his or her true partner, because too often we confuse physical attraction with true soul attraction. The cravings of the body are so strong that they may override the cravings of the soul. The expression "I've found the love of my life" is heard too routinely, and frequently it emerges that this "love" does not pass the reality test.

The separation of a true couple is a situation of negative cosmic imbalance caused by the accumulation of negative karma and the incomplete state of one or both partners. It is therefore incumbent upon us to aspire to eliminate negativity and balance our karma for the sake of ourselves and our partners. Each individual fills an important role in the cosmic unfolding, as the harmony of the universe is preserved through the balance of all of its parts.

The forming of a couple is a step taken to harness the power of both partners for the sake of advancing their spiritual enlightenment, and so that they may help one another to complete their restoration. Ideally, each will have previously gotten in touch with their male and female parts, united them, and achieved inner completion. The man should get in touch with his female side, and the woman should get in touch with her male side. Carl Jung called these unconscious properties *anima*, or the inner female in each man, and *animus*, the inner male in each woman.

The existence of the anima and the animus in every individual testifies to human beings' capacity to reach the longed-for inner completion. People who accept their inner partner as worthy and their entitlement will not need to search for their missing piece in others, and can instead pass on their completion as a gift to their partners, and to the entire cosmos.

According to the Kabbalah, most women achieve their state of *tikun* (restoration-repair-correction)[1] before men. Occasionally, even if the state of restoration releases a woman from the need to come back for another incarnation, she may come back voluntarily in order to aid her partner in his struggle for restoration. By the same token, if a man has had the good fortune to come together with his partner, yet failed to prove himself worthy of her, then he will be compelled to return to this world to engage in *tikun* with someone other than his true partner, who in turn will have to come back for another incarnation only in order to unite with him.

Yet true fulfillment is shared only with one's true partner. When two people are worthy of one another in terms of the level of development of their souls, and each achieves inner completion, then the two halves can reunite in this world. Partners who have found each other must then progress toward a common goal that will benefit all, thereby finding true happiness and fulfillment.

---

1. A translation of the Kabbalistic concept of *tikun*.

CHAPTER THREE

THE PAIRS OF SIGNS

And the Holy One, Blessed be He, said: Behold, my children:
Everything that I created, I created in pairs:
The heavens and the earth, the sun and the moon
Adam and Eve, this world and the World to Come.
Yet I am singular and unique in the world.

—Dvarim Rabba 2, Yalkut Shimoni—Va'Etchanan 6 (*Midrashim*)

The zodiac is a path of experience of the soul; the soul moves through it toward its destinies and purposes, consistent with patterns imprinted upon it in past lives. The purpose of karmic astrology is to identify these patterns and to help the individual to cut loose from old subconscious behaviors that may constitute obstacles along his or her path in this life.

A person tries to balance the entirety of his or her past lives by focusing on certain signs. Sometimes many attempts are needed in one sign for that sign's lesson to be internalized, and sometimes only a few attempts are needed, as the lesson of that sign is learned quickly. Therefore, every chart has its own distribution of planets in the various signs. In many birth charts, several planets are placed in one sign, in which case that sign is considered *emphasized*.

The lessons of each sign are multiple, as each of the signs serves as a mirror that reflects its opposing sign. The principle of polarity is a key one in astrology. According to Yin and Yang theory, every thing contains within it the seed of its opposite, which in astrological terms means that behind every sign "hides" its opposite. Opposing signs lie opposite each other on an axis, yet strive toward each other. The uniting of these opposites creates completion. As such, when a certain sign is emphasized in a chart, it is crucial that it be balanced by the qualities of its opposing sign. One goal that challenges each of us is that of adopting the positive qualities of each of the two signs on our axis, while avoiding the negative qualities.

One way to achieve balance and unity of opposites is through a partner, who projects qualities that are suppressed in us, or who embodies facets that are absent in us. Through contact with this "missing side," we can learn to adopt these qualities.

THE OPPOSITE SIGNS ARE:

Aries/Libra
Taurus/Scorpio
Gemini/Sagittarius
Cancer/Capricorn
Leo/Aquarius
Virgo/Pisces

THE ARIES/LIBRA AXIS

The karmic goal of this axis is to achieve balance between maximum expression of individualism and the total appeasement of others' and society's demands. This balance can be achieved by deepening one's understanding that it is not possible to achieve fulfillment without taking into account others' needs. On the other hand, healthy relations cannot develop when there is forfeiture of one's personal needs.

Aries
When Aries, a fire sign, is emphasized in a chart, the person is very aware of his or her uniqueness. The incarnating soul has just left behind the interim stage between this life and its previous life, where it was an integral part of the universal consciousness. Now it has once again entered earthly existence, where individuality is respected, and the soul

that has chosen to experience Aries has set as its goal to differentiate itself, or to become a separate entity.

Aries is a sign of beginnings, and in the karmic sense, a circle has closed and a daring surge forward has taken place. Yet the blessing is mixed: In its everyday life, Aries may be enthused when something is new, yet lose interest along the way. The drive for newness burns within Aries, yet when the newness has worn off, Aries are not always willing to finish what they've started. An awareness of this pitfall can enable them to harness their forces to complete the tasks that they have taken upon themselves.

The energies of the sign of Aries, which is ruled by Mars, aid in the development of the ego, the will, and the initiative, of selfhood and autonomy, of the ability to conduct one-self, and of primacy and individuality. Those influenced by these energies may express this sign negatively, by being egotistical, controlling, belligerent, arrogant, reckless, or tactless, all of which create negative karma; or they may choose to express these energies positively, learning to modulate these Aries forces, or to activate them, though not at the expense of others. Consideration for others can be learned from Aries' opposing sign, Libra, for whom it is a fundamental principle. It is incumbent upon Aries to also learn to moderate ambition and competitiveness, and to overcome impulsiveness and aggressive tendencies.

Negative karma is created mainly by improper use of the ego. While this is true of every sign, it is particularly so in Aries' case. Harnessing the ego to serve others' needs and expanding the boundaries of the "I" to include others can aid Aries in wiping out negative karma.

It is also incumbent upon Aries to work on building a self-image that is not based on creating an external impression, or on the need for others' admiration; rather, Aries' self-image should be founded on a genuine sense of self-worth that emanates from the primal energy flowing within.

Libra

The incarnating soul in Libra, a sign ruled by Venus, has reached this world in order to experience and bestow love, and to put into action the principle of consideration for others. Libras also use graciousness to advance the cooperation of which the Libra soul is so in need.

In the karmic sense, an emphasis on Libra shows that the individual has been given the opportunity to make amends for mistakes made in previous incarnations resulting from selfishness and lack of consideration. However, this time around, the Libra may develop a tendency to serve others' needs at any price. Therefore it is incumbent upon Libras to take care not to get to the point that they become a shadow of someone else, or experience life through others and are fed by their energies. Libras must avoid slipping into indecisiveness, complacence, and over-compromising, as the fear of standing behind one's principles and getting into conflicts with others can ultimately lead to the eclipse of one's own selfhood.

The karmic objective of Libras is to find the middle ground between their own and others' egos, and to flow toward seeing themselves as others' equals. In this way, Libra comes to embody its symbol—the scales—whose purpose is to reach perfect balance. Balance, however, is not automatic or instant, and Libras must learn to navigate such that the balance achieved is durable, because if it is disrupted, they may experience instability, a critical condition in their case.

Another Libra goal is to achieve the ability to see both sides of the coin in any situation while remaining objective. As such, Libras are occasionally accused of losing touch with feelings, remaining uninvolved, or not taking a stand. Indeed, in their drive to thoroughly examine an issue, Libras tend to reason coolly and to the point; in their zeal to judge an issue justly, they may over-apply intellect and cut themselves off from emotion.

As an air sign, Libras are practiced at the art of interpersonal communication, yet must also learn to communicate with themselves. A person with an emphasis on Libra must also learn not to be afraid of his or her dark side, which may emerge in the self-discovery process. Spiritual clarity is possible only once a person conducts a no-holds-barred dialog with him- or herself. Only then can one effectively fulfill one's supreme karmic purpose: to achieve balance within one's own soul, to achieve harmony with the cosmic forces, and to add to the welfare, justice, beauty, and harmony in the world.

THE TAURUS/SCORPIO AXIS

The karmic purpose of this axis is the consolidation of proper values and the correct attitude toward power and desire. The goal here is to harmoniously combine material values with spiritual ones; to develop the ability to use power, not to rule over or to destroy, but rather to build; and to use passion as an impetus for transcendence.

Taurus

The incarnating soul in Taurus, an earth sign, is keenly aware of the material, of property, of the body's urges, and of life's fundamental pleasures. When Taurus is emphasized in a chart, then in this incarnation the soul is here to compensate for a lack of physical and other charms that were its lot in past incarnations, and to fully experience the physical side of human existence.

Taurus aspires to achieve rest and relaxation. Taureans who are unevolved spiritually will fulfill this aspiration through collecting material goods. Taureans who have attained a high spiritual level interpret this aspiration metaphorically, and their karmic purpose to achieve tranquility and harmony is accompanied by a deep understanding that establishing their inherence is not conditional on economic or material gain.

One of Taurus's karmic lessons is to develop inner confidence and self-worth that do not derive from material value or surrounding objects. Taureans must activate the right degree of moderation to control their materialistic tendencies; otherwise, materialism will control them, and the attachment to things can become an obsession. Taurus is here to learn the lesson of satisfaction and gratification without greed, or the simple truth of the saying "Who is rich? He who is satisfied with his lot."

Taureans are stubborn and slow-moving, learning their lessons while they mobilize their prominent qualities of perseverance, endurance, thoroughness, moderation, patience, practicality, and loyalty. Taureans are disciplined and do not cut themselves any slack, yet they must learn when to move on; otherwise, they find themselves spinning their wheels.

Taurus is a "preserving" sign, which unfortunately also means "preserving" anger and grudges. Suppression of these feelings can lead to accumulating baggage and consequent disproportionate outbursts that are potentially self-destructive or destructive to one's surroundings. Therefore, it is important that Taureans learn to express their feelings before these feelings overpower their owners.

Taureans also preserve memories, and it is hard for them to shake loose from past experiences and move forward. Therefore, it is particularly difficult for them to break free of negative karma, and they may carry karmic burdens from previous incarnations, not understanding that the time has come to shed them. Taureans must therefore learn to distinguish between caution and fear, as fear of change can cause them to bind themselves to their routine and thus get stuck in a rut.

As they are ruled by Venus, Taureans must also learn to balance physical and spiritual love, as well as to perfect their capacity to give. It is incumbent upon Taureans to become virtuosos of love and giving, as through these, they can fulfill their karmic purpose.

Scorpio

Being a water sign, Scorpios use their inner powers acquired in past incarnations to dive into reality—both the hidden and the revealed—and stride without fear into areas of life that others consider taboo. Scorpios, being ruled by Pluto, do not make do with what is on the surface, but rather delve underneath; occasionally this results in their getting lost in the labyrinth of the subconscious.

Scorpios have deep, embedded feelings, of which they must learn to let go gradually, as holding onto them can cause a volcano-like eruption. Scorpios' vulnerability and the intensity of their feelings may be directed destructively toward others or toward themselves.

Scorpios have penetrating sight, and can see into the depths of others' psyches. As such, they must use their capacity to pierce, not as a knife with which to stab, but rather as a surgical instrument used to remove malignancies. Scorpios must mobilize this ability to help others, and not harm them by exposing others' Achilles' heels.

An individual whose chart is emphasized by Scorpio may be cynical, critical, suspicious, jealous, materialistic, coercive, or compulsive. Scorpio is also ruled by Mars, the god of war, so that Scorpios may often find themselves in conflict or strife, as their way of solving problems and molding their self-image is through grappling with conflict. Therefore, Scorpios' task is to learn to solve problems and discover their identity not through conflict, but rather by rising above it. There, from above, they can see the whole picture instead of the narrow plank on which they stand. Indeed, Scorpios can choose to live as reptiles—inhabiting the dark and nether regions, descending to the depths of sexuality, and letting their animal instincts take over; or they can become eagles, soaring to the heights on the wings of evolved spirituality.

Sexuality, mysticism, and death preoccupy Scorpios, who arrive in this incarnation to learn to use their sexual powers as a path to renewal and change, and to achieve the death of the ego through sexual union. An incarnating soul in Scorpio is here in order to transform the "inferno" of reincarnation into the purifying fire of this life. Therefore, yet another image associated with Scorpios is the phoenix, which is consumed by fire only to rise again. Likewise, incarnating souls in Scorpio can break free of the sins and vengeances of the past that have burdened them over many incarnations, and achieve transformation in all areas of life.

The karmic purpose of a soul embodied in a Scorpio is to pass from darkness into light, from the hidden paths and tunnels of the subconscious into the light of redemption of higher consciousness.

THE GEMINI/SAGITTARIUS AXIS

The karmic purpose of this axis is the blending of pure reason and broad faith, of the intellect and intuition, of practical knowledge and inner wisdom. This blending can be achieved through tuning in to the cosmic reservoir of knowledge and wisdom.

Gemini

The main activity of a soul incarnating in Gemini is gathering information and passing on knowledge. Those whose charts show an emphasis on Gemini own flexible minds and have the ability to adapt to changing circumstances. Their openness to ideas and knowledge aids them in abandoning rigid beliefs from past lives; yet at the same time, they may fall into the trap of superficiality, restlessness, inability to concentrate, and the search for new experiences before they have internalized what they have learned. Therefore, Geminis must discipline themselves, learn to calm their wandering minds, digest what they have learned, and continue forward. Only then can they free themselves up to absorb new material.

Gemini is ruled by Mercury, the quick-footed messenger of the gods. A typical Gemini is quick, alert, in constant motion, and young-minded. He or she is also colorful, a fast learner, chatty, and overly curious, and focuses on extraneous details. The saying "Grasp all, lose all" aptly describes the Gemini. Gemini's task is to learn from Sagittarius, its opposing sign, the art of comprehensive, synoptic vision.

The twins, Gemini's symbol, embody the duality of the universe, and duality lies at the foundation of Gemini's nature. Geminis have at least two personalities, each of which wants to be somewhere else, and each of which is occupied with taking in information from various sources. Therefore, Geminis must learn to clear their minds of scraps of unimportant information to make room for higher wisdom.

Geminis are sensitive to language and words, and because their main task is imparting knowledge, it is incumbent upon them to exploit this sensitivity, constantly perfecting their expressive skills. In addition, they must also work on developing their listening skills.

Geminis' most important karmic purpose is to learn the concept of unity in the spiritual sense. Internalizing this concept will aid them in gathering their personalities under the single roof of the completed self, thus achieving stability and peace.

Sagittarius

The incarnating soul with an emphasis on Sagittarius cherishes above all freedom and broadening one's horizons. Sagittarians are constantly on a quest for meaning, and must find a meaning and a significance for everything. Sagittarians expose the truth step by step, using their evolved intuition and their adherence to their goals. Sagittarians are eternal wanderers, moving constantly through physical, mental, and philosophical realms, and infecting those around them with their enthusiasm, optimism, and joie de vivre.

The spiritually evolved Sagittarian may have worked for many incarnations on gathering knowledge and tuning directly in to ancient wisdom. Through many existences, Sagittarians have served as spiritual teachers and transmitted their knowledge generously to others. The karmic plan of Sagittarius, a sign ruled by Jupiter, offers Sagittarians many possibilities for experiencing various realms, and as such they must activate their sense of proportion in order not to be dragged into excesses. They must also identify the essential from among the many opportunities that litter their paths.

On the other hand, Sagittarians who are not spiritually evolved may exploit their knowledge to control others. They may be hypocrites, overly pious, intolerant, arrogant, vulgar, or zealous. Sagittarius is symbolized by the centaur, or half man, half horse, who holds a drawn bow, his head in the sky and his feet on the ground. While this soul's purpose is to tune in to the absolute knowledge, when it takes flight into the infinite, it must take care not to forget the grounding of reality.

Experiencing the energies of this fire sign enables Sagittarians to transcend narrow horizons, jealousy, or obsession, as the goal of this incarnating soul is to act out of inspiration. It must look at everything philosophically, to absorb things holistically, to externalize feelings and knowledge, to expand, and to take flight to the spiritual heights.

THE CANCER/CAPRICORN AXIS

The karmic purpose of this axis is to achieve the integration of the inner male and the inner female, to find the balance between softness and hardness, and to resolve the conflict between the demands of family and career, the personal and the public. Respect for tradition and the past is prominent in this axis.

Cancer

The soul embodied in the sign of Cancer is in touch with the archetypal female and maternal qualities, or the eternal nurturing energy of the Great Mother. An important lesson for Cancers is learning to distinguish between mothering and smothering. Cancer is loyal, devoted, and protected, and must learn when to protect and when to let go, when to nurture and when to give space to loved ones.

Emotional security may in itself constitute a supreme goal for Cancer, because alongside its desire to protect, Cancer has a strong need to create a protective wall around itself. A lack of confidence and emotional shortcomings can cause Cancer to demand constant attention. Cancers may use their evolved imaginations to exaggerate their feelings of deprivation and create imagined situations wherein they play the role of the chronically deprived. In order to bolster their emotional confidence, Cancers may collect goods, or become attached to money or to people. In addition, Cancers may be needy, sucking the energy of those under whose wings they have chosen to take refuge.

Cancers are sentimental and cling to the past. As a water sign, they experience the world mainly through the spectrum of their feelings. As Cancer is ruled by the Moon, which is constantly changing, Cancers are given to emotional extremes and moodiness, even absorbing the emotions of others.

Souls that choose to be embodied as a Cancer have done so in order to experience emotional intensity that was withheld from them in past incarnations. Cancers don't always know how to handle this intensity, so their lesson is to learn to balance feelings. When Cancers learn to balance their energies and express them positively, then they are warm and sensitive without using coercion or emotional blackmail; they succeed in extending the right degree of protection to others.

Capricorn

The goal of an incarnating soul in the sign of Capricorn is to establish self-discipline and true authority. In Capricorn, the soul comes into contact with the energies of the archetypal father, or the omnipotent god, and learns to internalize these energies and exploit them. Saturn, known as the god of karma, rules Capricorn, so that the incarnating soul in this sign is super-aware of both limitations imposed upon it and karmic debts that it is compelled to pay off by the very fact of its existence in this world.

Souls who incarnate in Capricorn may feel a heavy sense of restriction, introversion, and subjugation. They see the world through the lens of payoff and penalty, and as such weigh every step cautiously. This caution is desirable as long as it does not cause a fear of failure to overtake them, and as long as it does not prevent them from achieving self-fulfillment.

Like the mountain goat, the symbol of Capricorn, which overcomes obstacles on its path and steadily makes its way to the yearned-for summit, Capricorns—an earth sign—climb with perseverance, ambition, and uncompromising discipline toward the goals that they set for themselves. Capricorns are indefatigable in their pursuit to achieve their goals and must learn to rein in their ambitiousness, as their overconfident climbing could end in a fall. Capricorns aspire to reach a high status in society, yet if they get there without having worked on their self-esteem, they tend to tyrannize those subordinate to them, to gather possessions, and to adopt symbols of power in an attempt to earn honor and prestige. Therefore Capricorns must work on believing in themselves and developing self-confidence. The present incarnation gives them the opportunity to achieve respect as responsible, practical, trustworthy, reasonable, and authoritative human beings.

Capricorns' opposing sign, Cancer, can be an example for them of softness and sensitivity. Capricorns must learn to identify and eliminate the hindrances and obstructions imprinted upon them in previous incarnations, to round their sharp edges, and to moderate their demands of themselves and others. Otherwise, they will form walls of alienation and isolation around themselves. They must also learn the difference between suppressing the self, which blocks self-development, and self-discipline, which leads to real and lasting achievements. Thus, they can break free of the dogmatism that is the lot of unevolved Capricorns, and expand their world to include spirituality and vision.

THE LEO/AQUARIUS AXIS

In this axis, the karmic goal is to establish the values of love and creative power. This goal can be achieved by expanding one's personal circle of love and practicing altruism, as well as by integrating the demands of the individual and the demands of the community. The concept of creativity in this axis takes on an all-encompassing significance of both artistic creativity and giving birth to ideas, and literal creativity, or procreation.

Leo
The soul incarnating in Leo embodies life's creative side, and the karmic task here is to establish inner strength and radiate it outward for the good of all, with nobility, joy, and

love. Leos must develop their authoritativeness by finding esteem within themselves, and not expect to get it from others.

Unevolved Leos need constant stroking and praise, and behave in an exhibitionist manner to impress and receive applause. Leos are attracted to fame, glory, and drama. Instead of being prisoners of their glittery outer image, they need to develop the inner power and splendor of the Sun, which rules this sign.

For Leos, hedonism and extravagance can become a way of life. Leos must therefore learn to enjoy life without slipping into wanton hedonism. Leos, like all of the fire signs, have big egos, and must learn to rein in their controlling tendencies and their craving for respect and, above all, avoid hubris, or the sin of pride.

An emphasis on Leo in one's chart shows that the individual has mastered in past lives the qualities of the signs that precede it in the zodiac: the leadership of Aries, the can-do capacity of Taurus, the curiosity of Gemini, and the sensitivity and generosity of Cancer. Therefore, Leos' karmic task is to perfect and apply these qualities for the good of all, which they can learn from Aquarius, their opposing sign. This can be achieved by leading without arrogance, being strong and authoritative without being controlling, communicating and being sensitive to others' needs, giving without expecting admiration in return, and giving of themselves while tuning in to the power of universal love.

Aquarius

The incarnating soul with an emphasis on Aquarius has come into this world to implement ideas in a unique way: to change, repair, and break free of the boundaries of the past. The karmic purpose here is to blaze new, original, and unconventional trails, even when it entails a certain degree of nonconformism and rebellion against conventions. As Aquarius's symbol is the water bearer, and its ruling planet is Uranus, one of Aquarius's functions is bringing light to humanity and linking humanity to the higher worlds. Therefore, Aquarius's karmic task is to absorb and shed cosmic light on the human race.

Humanity is now in the Age of Aquarius, in which spirituality, equality, and fellowship are held in esteem. The karmic purpose is to achieve fellowship not only between people, but also with the Creation; thus, the term "political correctness" is applicable at this time. Equality and fellowship are important to Aquarians, and their love for humanity is expressed through reform and innovation for the sake of improving society as a whole.

Because their eyes are fixed on humanity, Aquarians find casual relationships—wherein feelings can be put aside—easier to maintain than personal relationships, which demand emotional involvement. Therefore, Aquarians must learn to balance between the personal and the impersonal.

Aquarians are on a familiar footing with the new, the futuristic, and an alternative understanding of life; their entire beings are tuned in to the future. Therefore, they have no problem leaving behind old beliefs. At the same time, when Aquarius energies are expressed negatively, it can lead to "rebellion without a cause" and to trampling on tradition for its own sake. Aquarius, an air sign, also has a tendency to get carried away with ideals and ignore the limitations of reality, which can lead to the smashing of dreams.

An evolved soul incarnating in Aquarius comes into this world to learn to progress with unbiased self-examination. Original thought processes, resourcefulness and inventiveness, the ability to cut loose from the ego, intellectual curiosity, and objectivity all enable Aquarians not only to direct their inspiration toward their own development, but also to achieve their karmic task of developing and improving the human race.

THE VIRGO/PISCES AXIS

The karmic purpose of this axis is to blend the world beyond with the here and now, to develop analytical abilities, and to sharpen both focused and wide vision in order to see both the forest and the trees. Above all, the overarching karmic goal of this axis is to serve humanity.

Virgo

Incarnating souls in Virgo offer the world their desire to serve with humility and suppression of the ego. This soul searches for quality, not quantity. It comes into this world to scrutinize reality, to take responsibility, and to work toward inner and outer purity.

The purification of the soul is achieved through hard work with no expectation of reward or thanks, through engaging in the therapy or treatment professions, or through illnesses that the Virgo overcomes. Through dealing with illness—either as a practitioner or a patient—the strong need to understand the body-mind connection is fulfilled. On the other hand, the negative manifestation of this path lies in a preoccupation with the body, which can lead to hypochondria or fanaticism in the health realm, such as extreme diets or self-mortification. Because teaching is a no less important karmic task for the Virgo, this dimension occasionally takes on a shade of preachiness, so that Virgos may end up proselytizing for their chosen cause.

Individuals with an emphasis on Virgo come into this world to learn to perfect everything that they do, yet the search for perfection can cause them to lose perspective, leading to obsessive-compulsive behaviors, pedanticism, detail obsession, and a failure to see the whole picture.

Balance is always the name of the game, and Virgos must aspire to perfection while learning to be satisfied with less. Virgos who fail to internalize this balance may suffer from feelings of inferiority or frustration or of being overlooked. They cannot be satisfied because their demands of themselves and others are so high. Therefore, learning to accept imperfection is a karmic task no less important than the aspiration to perfection.

The task of Virgos, a sign ruled by Mercury, the planet of mental processes, is also to perfect the art of analysis and logic. In addition to all of this, Virgos must learn to rein in their critical nature, both toward themselves and others, and to remember that their will to express themselves logically may sabotage their emotional side. Virgos must learn to tune in to the lighter side of life, to transform their characteristic cynicism and irony into humor, and to learn from Pisces, their opposing sign, how to go with the flow.

Pisces

Pisces is the last sign in the zodiac, and when the soul incarnates with an emphasis on Pisces, it may be in a final stage of an incarnational cycle. Because Pisces is ruled by Neptune, Pisces' tendency is to break out of the material world and fulfill their spiritual longing to unite with the cosmos. When the soul has already experienced the gamut of experiences in the material and earthly realms, it is ready to soar to the spiritual realms. When the incarnating soul embodies the positive side of Pisces, it places a premium on unconditional love, altruism, and rising above the material world. The denial of the worldly and the suppression of the ego are goals that the Piscean incarnating soul can achieve here and now.

People born under Pisces are creative, highly sensitive to their surroundings, and have telepathic perception. Yet these abilities have the potential to overwhelm them, because they have a tendency to take in all of the information without sorting it. Occasionally, Pisceans absorb the emotions of others, and at other times, they may absorb events from a previous existence as if they were being experienced now. Pisces' sensitivity enables them to tune in to their surroundings, whether to fulfill artistic needs or to fulfill others' needs. At the same time, this sensitivity may be accompanied by vulnerability, which in turn could lead to escapism, or the desire to run away from a disappointing reality into a world of one's own creating.

Escapism may manifest in addictions, but could also manifest in daydreaming or the tendency to sleep for an inordinate amount of time. Another form of escapism is the phenomenon of losing focus, or getting caught up in illusions. Therefore, the karmic task of a soul reborn as a Pisces is to learn to stay focused and to relate to the here and now. Pisceans must also develop the ability to discern, which is the strong point of Virgo, Pisces' opposing sign. The evolved Pisces must tune in to reality, because only then can he or she freely soar to the spiritual realms, see inner reason, and apply spiritual significance to everyday matters.

Sign	Symbol	Ruling Planet	Symbol
Aries	♈	Mars	♂
Taurus	♉	Venus	♀
Gemini	♊	Mercury	☿
Cancer	♋	Moon	☽
Leo	♌	Sun	☉
Virgo	♍	Mercury	☿
Libra	♎	Venus	♀
Scorpio	♏	Pluto, Mars	♇, ♂
Sagittarius	♐	Jupiter	♃
Capricorn	♑	Saturn	♄
Aquarius	♒	Uranus, Saturn	♅, ♄
Pisces	♓	Neptune, Jupiter	♆, ♃

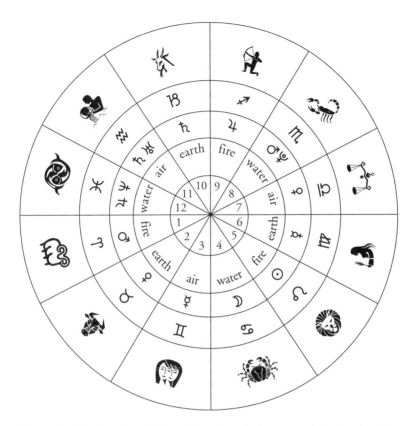

Figure 1—The Symbols, Ruling Planets, and Elements of the Twelve Signs

CHAPTER FOUR

THE PLANETS AND
KARMIC RELATIONSHIPS

In all of the planets and constellations of all of the heavens,
Governors and clerks have been appointed to serve the world,
Each and every one as is fitting.
Not even a blade of grass exists in all the world
That is not controlled by a planet and a constellation in the heavens . . .

—ZOHAR, PART 2, FOLIO 171

In a birth chart analyzed from a karmic point of view, the planets, like the rest of the factors in the chart, indicate qualities whose origins lie in past incarnations. Each planet in a chart has some significance to past lives, and likewise each planet plays a role in the person's present life. The task of the owner of the chart is to overcome the negative conditioning represented by the planets, and to incorporate their positive traits into the present, on the new path taken by the incarnating soul.

In karmic astrology, the planets are divided into personal planets and karmic planets:

- The **Sun, Moon, Mercury, Venus,** and **Mars** are *personal planets*. Being the inner planets, they reveal to us the basic personality of an individual and the traits that the person should develop in this incarnation.

- **Saturn**, **Uranus**, **Neptune**, and **Pluto** are *karmic planets*. Being the outer planets, they are tied to those circumstances beyond our control, which represent the karmic burden that a person brings into this world.

- **Jupiter** is between the two groups of planets, and serves as an intercessor. As the planet of good fortune, expansion, and optimism, Jupiter bestows the best on a personality and moderates negative karmic influences.

It should be noted that a karmic planet is considered a personal planet when it rules the *Ascendant*, or *rising sign*. The rising sign is the sign in which a chart opens, and it represents the owner of this chart, or *the native*. If, for example, Scorpio is the rising sign, then Pluto, which is considered a karmic planet, automatically becomes the personal planet of this individual, together with Mars. If the rising sign is Aquarius, then Uranus becomes the personal planet, together with Saturn. In these cases, Pluto and Uranus represent both the individual's personality and the karmic influences affecting the person.

A planet is manifested in a chart both by its placement in a house and sign, and by its aspects, i.e., its relationships—either harmonious or disharmonious—with the other planets. The positioning of the planets in a chart is chosen by the soul and creates a unique energetic pattern that indicates both choices made in the past and potential choices, enabling the incarnating soul to balance its previous incarnations.

When two planets are at a distance of 60° or 120° from each other, they are in a harmonious relationship. When two planets are at a distance of 90° or 180° from each other, they are in a disharmonious relationship. *Aspects* are the distances between the planets, and they are measured in degrees. The aspects represent the way a planet's energy is manifested, or the nature of its energetic influence in the two chart.

In general, it can be said that *harmonious aspects* in a chart indicate smoothly flowing planetary energy, and are therefore also referred to as flowing aspects. The *disharmonious aspects* reveal problem areas and obstacles, struggles and conflicts. They are therefore considered difficult aspects, yet are also considered dynamic and challenging, as they prod and urge us to act and to evolve. Additional information on aspects can be found in appendix B.

With respect to karma, harmonious aspects in a chart indicate past problems that have been resolved, or problem areas that have been worked on in past incarnations. This person learned the lesson, finally achieving understanding at the end of a past life or in the interim between the last life and this one. In the present life, this person is successfully incorporating the lesson.

Disharmonious aspects show that the struggle to achieve the goals represented by the planets forming the aspect was not resolved in the previous incarnation. There remain obstacles on the path to fulfillment that the person has still not managed to overcome, and with which the individual must still grapple in this life.

A person is not always aware of inner conflicts. Relationships can accelerate the process of gaining awareness, because those involved reflect each other's problems, so that we actually encounter ourselves in others. This encounter with another enables us to step back from ourselves and see things objectively, thus reflecting karmic problems that we must work on.

When we examine a person's relationships by comparing his or her chart to other people's charts, the first step is to survey the aspects formed between personal planets in the two charts. This shows the compatibility or lack thereof between the two partners. However, in order to understand the karmic connection between them, we must focus on aspects formed between personal planets in one chart and karmic planets in the other. These aspects represent certain facets of the karmic history of the partners as manifested in the present incarnation. The more aspects formed between the two charts, the more significant is their shared karmic history.

Flowing aspects represent harmonious relationship patterns, and the challenging aspects indicate negative behavior patterns established in the relationship. These disharmonious aspects actually represent the karmic bonds that bind the two souls to one another, and their examination reveals conflicts between them. These conflicts must be resolved; otherwise, it is impossible to break the bonds with this other soul.

The outer, or karmic, planets play the active role in the relationship. They exert an influence that is absorbed by the personal planets, and actually serve as stimulators. When two people meet again in a new incarnation, the encounter of the personal planet with the karmic planet arouses in the partner represented by the personal planet behavior patterns from previous lives, stimulating him or her to act in order to break free of these patterns.

The personal-planet partner feels a strong attraction to the karmic-planet partner. Even if the relationship causes the former actual discomfort or problems, he or she finds it difficult to end it. The personal-planet partner has an emotional need to continue the relationship, and only when the lesson from it has been learned and internalized can he or she break free of destructive behaviors and the karmic bond, make needed repairs, and balance the shared karma.

In comparing charts, a planet in one chart influences the other chart particularly when:

- it forms many aspects with planets from the second chart.
- it falls in a significant house in the second chart.
- it is in *conjunction* with a significant planet in the second chart.

The conjunction aspect is key in examining relationships, and therefore a separate chapter is devoted to it.

THE SUN

In a birth chart, the Sun represents the unique identity that we wish to realize in the present existence. The Sun also represents the ego, which is the force that directs us toward our goals, and which drives us to leave our imprint on the world. As such, the Sun shows us our direction and the primary goal that we've set for ourselves in this incarnation. It represents the conscious, the qualities that we try to develop here and now, self-expression, creativity, ambition, and the desire for recognition and esteem.

Understanding the energies of a given Sun sign and the nature of its manifestation in a chart enables us to see clearly the means of reinforcing our positive qualities and working on the negative. This understanding also illuminates the path to a true integration of all parts of the personality.

When comparing charts, the Sun's influence from one chart on another chart shows how and in what area the will and self-expression of the Sun individual influences the partner. The Sun's influence can be either beneficial or thwarting, as it reveals and illuminates both good and bad qualities.

The Sun also represents authority, and as such it symbolizes the authority figures in a person's life, as well as anyone who acts as a father figure. These paternal figures may operate protectively and supportively, or conversely they may be overbearing and dictatorial. Either one may be the case; thus the Sun's influence causes the partner to demonstrate positive power and self-expression and to "shine" with full potential; or alternatively, the partner may perceive the Sun's influence as a threat, and it may "dim" his or her own light and minimize his or her self-image.

The Sun's influence is always accompanied by a certain degree of a show of power. When an aspect involving the Sun also involves a karmic planet, and the aspect is manifested disharmoniously, subconscious memories of a father or father figure who exposed the person's weaknesses, causing hurt, will be aroused in the person influenced by the Sun. Contact with the Sun will arouse subconscious fears or hurt from past incarnations, and a need for self-protection, any of which can block life forces and self-expression.

THE MOON

Just as the sun and moon are the two most significant celestial bodies for those of us inhabiting Earth, so are the Sun and Moon in the birth chart dominant in the soul's present life, and are likewise important. Jung attributed the powers of the Sun to the male archetype, and the powers of the Moon to the female archetype; thus the Sun and the Moon represent the classic polarity between the *yang*, or the active, influential, male essence, and the *yin*, or the passive and receptive female essence. As such, the Sun symbolizes the patron father, while the Moon symbolizes the nurturing and protecting mother, as well as the home and family. In nature, the moon reflects the sun's light, so that astrologically speaking, the Moon represents the principle of reception and response. This principle in turn symbolizes the emotions and one's capacity to sense and to reflect the moods and needs of others; thus the Moon is also identified with care and sympathy.

In addition, the Sun represents the present, and the Moon, the past. The Moon reflects what a person was in the past, whether in this incarnation or in the overall past of the soul. The Moon represents the gamut of experiences, memories, impressions, and habits of the past, as well as patterns and behaviors that come naturally to a person. We feel comfortable with these patterns immediately upon birth, because they are already familiar to us, having been rooted in our subconscious.

The Moon shows us the roots of our self-image. It expresses the incarnating soul's deepest needs for security, as well as the means by which the soul searches to fill this need. It also expresses our instinctive reactions and the ways in which we automatically protect ourselves.

The Moon represents the subconscious, while the Sun represents the conscious. As such, an astrological look at the relationship between them (for example, the degree of compatibility between their signs and the aspects between them) shows the degree of a person's capacity to integrate the conscious self and the subconscious self. This integration is what contributes to the completeness of the personality.

The karmic contacts of the Moon are the most significant, meriting particular attention. In comparing charts, the relationship of the Moon in one chart to factors in the other chart shows how a person reacts to contact with others, and whether this contact sets into motion karmic mental and emotional patterns that either drag the person down or aid attempts at self-expression and adaptation to his or her surroundings.

Harmonious contact shows that a person responds instinctively, without restricting emotions to disrupt the contact, while disharmonious contact shows that he or she restricts and suppresses the expression of emotions or, conversely, overreacts.

When, in comparing two charts, we see that the Moon in one chart falls in a significant place in the other, forming many aspects with both karmic planets and personal planets, it is clear testimony to the fact that in a past incarnation there was a close family relationship between these two people.

If the aspects between the two charts are mostly harmonious, then the two individuals have met up again in this incarnation in order to continue to support each other emotionally and enjoy each other. If the contact between the charts is disharmonious, it shows that the relationship in this life was renewed in order to give the two people an opportunity to resolve familial conflicts whose roots lie deep in a past incarnation.

MERCURY

Mercury represents the intellect, rational thought, learning aptitude, speech, and language. Communication in all its forms is also ruled by Mercury. This planet represents the urge to communicate through the spoken or written word, and its location in a chart shows whether this is achieved easily or with difficulty. Its location likewise shows the approach of a person to acquiring knowledge. Mercury is also associated with adaptability and change, variety, speed, and a youthful mentality.

From a karmic point of view, Mercury's activity in a chart is exerted on the processes leading to karmic balance. Mercury shows how a person used Mercury-ruled talents in past incarnations, and how he or she can continue to exploit these talents to progress toward goals in this life and to repair what needs to be repaired.

An individual ruled by Mercury is an eternal student, and Mercury's aspects with karmic planets show the nature of the relations with those who taught him or her in the past. A disharmonious karmic aspect may remind the native of a teacher or other adult who caused him or her to feel inferior, arousing bitterness and distrust. Yet all the aspects of Mercury point in the direction of how the native can continue effectively learning in this life.

In comparing two charts, Mercury's influence shows the nature of mental connections and the level of communication between the two people. When Mercury's aspects with planets in the second chart are harmonious, then communication flows, and words are absorbed and interpreted as they are meant.

Harmonious aspects between Mercury and karmic planets show productive and beneficial communication that existed between the two partners in past lives. The karmic-planet partner helps the Mercury partner to shape his or her thought patterns and to open blocked communication processes.

Conversely, Mercury's disharmonious aspects with planets in the second chart can block communication. The Mercury individual may feel that the partner does not listen, does not understand, or does not process correctly what is said, in turn causing the person to lose trust in communication with the partner.

In such a case, the karmic-planet partner may try to pressure the Mercury partner, creating resistance that in turn causes verbal conflicts. The karmic-planet partner may disrupt the emotional calm of the Mercury partner, causing problems that existed between them in past incarnations to resurface.

There are cases wherein an encounter with another arouses in us a sense of familial closeness. Mercury also represents those to whom we are or were related, such as a sibling or close cousin. In this case, we should look for aspects between Mercury and karmic planets, and whether there are other elements that indicate a family relationship, such as aspects formed with the third or fourth houses, or with planets in those houses. When such conditions exist, we are seeing a renewed encounter with a relative from a past incarnation.

VENUS

While all planets play a part in our understanding of relationships, Venus is a central participant in every relationship, ruling all relationships, whether a romantic, social, or business partnership. Venus represents the urge to get to know others, the will to establish sharing and cooperation, and the desire to experience joy and pleasure. Venus also represents the social urge for mutual growth.

Venus embodies the capacity to love and be loved, as well as our desire to attract others to us with charm and a pleasing appearance. Behind the emotional desires of Venus is the longing that lies at the foundation of human nature: the need to unite with one's other half.

Beyond embodying love and sensitivity, Venus represents values, revealing here both of its faces: the abstract and the tangible. Venus is associated with beauty, aesthetics, justice, art, and culture on the one hand, and with material values such as money, property, and the need for security on the other.

Venus's location in a chart shows to what extent the person can find both financial and inner security, harmony, and peace of mind in this life, and the means at his or her disposal to achieve these. In addition, it shows the person's capacity to attract people, and what he or she needs to do in order to improve the chances of finding true love in this incarnation.

In comparing charts, when Venus in one chart forms aspects with personal planets in another chart, it shows the degree of emotional or romantic compatibility between the two natives. Even disharmonious aspects with personal planets in the other chart indicate love and warmth between the two, yet in such a case jealousy, possessiveness, or over-sensitivity may also exist, weighing on the relationship.

Venus's aspects with karmic planets in the other chart show a strong relationship between the two in past incarnations, and the nature of the aspects shows the degree of ease or difficulty in balancing or repairing past ties between the partners.

If the aspects are positive, contact will be relaxed, pleasant, and beneficial; while negative aspects express love-hate or approach-avoidance phenomena in the relationship. Jealousy, selfishness, criticism, or grudges may exist here, and occasionally a negative aspect indicates relations that are preoccupied with sensuality or sexuality, or those wherein there are conflicts over money.

Disharmonious aspects can indicate that such negative patterns have continued over several incarnations, and that it will be hard to overcome them in a single incarnation.

When a person learns to use the higher energies of Venus to bring the functions represented by Venus into balance, he or she can reach the heights of human expression, derive the maximum benefit from every connection, and achieve inner peace in all areas of life.

MARS

While the main attributes of Venus, a female planet, are cooperation and attraction, the main attribute of Mars is the consolidation of the ego; it "banishes" all others, lest they get in its way. Mars is a male planet, and sees the others as adversaries or competitors that thwart its freedom and the successful completion of its plans.

Mars represents energy, action, exertion, power, urges, drives, ability, and will, as well as individuality. With respect to karma, Mars's location in a chart shows how the person achieved his or her will, and his or her activities in the previous incarnation, as well as the extent of the person's efforts to advance and progress toward the fulfillment of goals in this incarnation.

Mars's location shows the means available to the person to work toward breaking energy blockages that may manifest destructively, so that the individual can actualize the positive, constructive side of his or her energy, power, and ability to perform.

Mars is a dynamic planet, and in chart comparison, its aspects with planets in the other chart show in what way and in what area it influences the partner. Its aspects show whether Mars spurs and stimulates the partner positively and constructively, or in a negative, annoying way.

Harmonious aspects with Mars enable the partner to discover his or her identity rapidly and directly, with no "side effects." However, when Mars contacts are disharmonious, the partner feels threatened, because Mars does not whitewash the truth; it attacks openly and forcefully.

The disharmonious aspects of Mars with karmic planets in the other chart bring out the worst in both partners, bringing to the surface negative patterns from the past that must be confronted head-on. However, harmonious aspects show cooperation in the past that could continue and gather momentum in the present.

In the case of romantic partners, the physical attraction that existed between them in a previous incarnation will flare up again, and the two can experience an energetic awakening that spreads to other areas.

JUPITER

Jupiter represents expansion and is associated with prosperity, luck, opportunities, success, optimism, and generosity. In addition, it represents broad knowledge, abstract and philosophical thinking, religion, morals, and the pursuit of justice. In fact, Jupiter's Hebrew name, *tzedek*, means "justice."

Karmically, Jupiter's activity in a chart cushion's one's path and eases the difficulties that stem from karmic situations, or those over which the person has no control in this life. Jupiter's position shows all of the "merit points" that a person has accumulated in past lives. It also symbolizes the degree of charity that will be activated in this life, and shows from what direction the person's goodness will emerge.

Jupiter is benefic; thus when its karmic influence is examined, we naturally focus on its positive influence. Yet when Jupiter manifests disharmoniously in a chart, it shows that the person goes overboard, which may bring about undesirable results due to overconfidence, excessive optimism, and blind faith in luck instead of sound judgment. Such a person must internalize the meaning of the law of karma: karma is not simply fate, but rather a law of cause and effect. While we may get lucky occasionally, we cannot rely on luck, and if we do, we waste the credit in our "good karma account."

Disharmonious aspects formed by Jupiter and karmic planets show how the person erred in the past, and also spurs the person to change philosophies and deepen his or her insight.

The same applies regarding aspects between Jupiter and personal or karmic planets in the other chart. When Jupiter forms disharmonious aspects, the partner may succumb to reckless, irresponsible behavior. Yet harmonious aspects arouse in the partner inner wisdom, encouraging spiritual development, affirming Jupiter's ancient reputation as the Greater Benefic.

SATURN

Saturn is considered a heavy and serious planet that represents the less pleasant aspects of life, such as obligations, difficulties, restrictions, and discipline. It is no surprise, therefore, that Saturn is associated more than any other planet with karma; indeed it is known as the Lord of Karma.

Karma actually means taking responsibility for our deeds, and as we know, this is not always easy. While difficult karma may be an opportunity for learning and development, or "making lemonade out of lemons," Saturn need not be perceived as a threat. Saturn simply represents the obstacles that litter the path to one's ultimate goal, as well as the means that can help us to strive and reach that goal.

Saturn is also known as the Great Teacher, because a teacher imposes upon us responsibility and discipline, and hard work so that we will learn and develop. By the same token, Saturn represents opportunities for growth and learning things that we have neglected or ignored in past incarnations. A person who clings to familiar patterns from the past, and who does not exploit opportunities to move forward, grow, and develop, needs a tough teacher like Saturn who will force him or her to meet the challenge of filling his or her deepest needs. If the person does not learn to do this quickly enough, and does not discover this on his or her own, then the hand of fate will take over.

Saturn represents intense experiences and learning that can take place only in the physical world and within a physical body. Pain, tension, and stress can actually cause us to develop and reach spiritual heights, as expressed in Exodus 1:13: "But the more they afflicted them, the more they multiplied and the more they spread abroad." Saturn's pressure should be accepted gratefully, because it causes us to do the hard work required for self-development.

Saturn is also associated with time, and is linked with the mythological god Cronus, the god of time who shows no mercy. Time therefore lies at the foundation of the law of karma, as issues do not always get resolved in a single incarnation. Hundreds or even thousands of years may pass before a person succeeds in paying off his or her karmic debts and achieving balance.

"There's no teacher like experience" is also a saying that expresses well Saturn's function. A person upon whom Saturn has a positive influence has amassed experience and achieved maturity and understanding of the ways of the world. The qualities that are typical of such a person are seriousness, caution, practical knowledge, conservativeness, responsibility, efficiency, modesty, and the ability to make do with little.

Yet Saturn's negative influence is manifested in rigidity, hesitancy, shrinking from newness and change, fears, and guilt feelings imprinted upon the soul from previous incarnations. In addition, in this incarnation, Saturn's negative influence is manifested in emotional suppression and blockages.

In comparing the charts of partners whose relationship is significant, Saturn's influence is conspicuous. Saturn's presence in long-term relationships is essential, as it is heavily associated with time and represents the long term or those things that withstand the test of time. There is no long-term relationship—whether romantic, business, or friendship—that is not influenced by Saturn.

Any given relationship that does not have at least one aspect with Saturn will not have a deep effect on the lives of either of the partners. Such a situation may signal that the relationship in question will not last.

When Saturn's influence is definitive, commitment lies in wait at the beginning of the relationship, both threatening and beckoning at the same time. Many times, fear of involvement characterizes the beginning of such a relationship, as one or both partners may sense that there is a karmic obligation that must be fulfilled. This sense may give way to subconscious holding back or withdrawal early on. Yet because karma demands its due, we cannot avoid such a relationship, and must enter into this commitment and meet the challenge.

There may be one of two reasons for Saturn's involvement in a relationship: either the Saturn individual has a continuing obligation from the past that must be fulfilled now, or the Saturn individual has avoided the obligation totally, and now the obligation must be carried out. In either case, this contact shows a debt not paid off; otherwise the relationship would not occur.

If Saturn's aspects are harmonious, then its influence on the chart is positive, and the relationship bestows upon the partners a sense of inner security, stability, loyalty, and mutual respect and responsibility.

The Saturn individual inspires in the partner a feeling of parenting and supportive authority, like a tough yet loving teacher who adheres to his or her principles. One can learn from such a teacher responsibility and discipline, organization and efficiency; yet the relationship is smooth, criticism is constructive, and there is no pressure to meet certain standards or expectations.

When Saturn is manifested disharmoniously, the Saturn individual can be a narrow-minded, rigid, and restrictive teacher, exploiting the partner's weakness in order to criticize, scorn, or oppress. One cannot learn from such a teacher, because the teacher employs fear, oppression, and punishments, and does not respect pupils' rights. As a result, feelings of bitterness, resentment, and chilliness will arise.

The authoritativeness of the Saturn partner is weighty, and he or she can make bad use of it. When the other person begins to grow and develop, the Saturn partner feels insecure, as if the reins are being taken out of his or her hands. In reaction, the Saturn partner may tyrannize the other and pull the reins even tighter. If he or she does not loosen up, the other may rebel and buck. On the other hand, if the Saturn partner chooses to cut the other person some slack, then he or she may be able to supervise fondly from afar, giving support yet not choking the partner.

In every case of a relationship with a strong Saturn influence, the bonds of obligation and loyalty bind the two together. The Saturn partner feels obligated to the other, and is concerned for him or her. Until the Saturn partner fulfills his or her karmic obligation to the other, he or she cannot rest. However, the Saturn person must learn to do this without binding the partner.

When Saturn in one chart influences another chart, it embodies the limitations of the influenced person, as well as the fears that he or she has not yet overcome. When he or she learns this and overcomes his or her limitations, the person can break free of the Saturnian influence, and the karma between the partners can reach a balance.

URANUS

Uranus is associated with all things irregular and unconventional, rebellion, nonconformity, changes, and inventions. In a karmic sense, Uranus's activity is manifested in breaking out of patterns from past incarnations and paving a new path. Uranus is known as the Great Emancipator, the Awakener, or the Enlightener, and its role is to change a person's mindset, worldview, and lifestyle, enabling the person to move forward to a new reality. Usually, Uranus's activity is sudden and unexpected, and therefore it is not always easy to absorb its effects.

Uranus's location in a birth chart shows whether the person is capable of coping with its energies and accepting change that ultimately brings about growth, or, conversely, whether the person fears or resists change, in which case Uranus's influence would manifest in a life crisis.

Uranus's influence brings with it the expansion of consciousness, which in turn manifests, among other phenomena, in introducing new experiences into our lives. As such, relations influenced by Uranus are founded on mutual discovery.

Uranus enables discovery and revelation of the unique sides of each partner. The Uranian contact causes them to feel that they are special, that the encounter between them is unique, tending to make their first encounter full of excitement.

Therefore, in Uranus-influenced relationships, each partner learns from the other how to express his or her uniqueness without limits, each partner functioning as a separate entity. Uranus's karmic gift is the ability to change one's outlook on life and break free of limits.

The Uranus partner needs freedom, and is extreme in his or her need for independence. Imprinted on his or her subconscious is the fear of losing that freedom, and therefore he or she guards it zealously. When Uranus is manifested disharmoniously, the Uranus partner may have a problem with intimacy; not only is it hard for this person to relate intimately to the partner, but he or she is not sensitive to the partner's needs.

While the Uranus individual does not force him- or herself on the partner—a strong point of the relationship—this habit can stem from aloofness or from unwillingness to commit to the relationship. It is impossible to predict when this person will be there and when he or she will be absent. Such a situation may cause the partner to feel insecurity or a fear of abandonment, and ultimately indifference to the relationship.

When Uranus's contact with the other chart is harmonious, the joy of the Uranus partner is in teaching the other partner the meaning of freedom and independent thinking. The Uranus partner supports and encourages the other on the path to self-growth. Because the partner cannot develop a dependence on the Uranus individual, his or her independence grows, and he or she accepts lovingly the separation between them.

When Uranus influences a relationship, it shows the recurrence of a discontinuous, unstable, and unanticipated relationship pattern from a previous incarnation. Usually this demonstrates an inability on the part of the two people to stabilize their relationship due to karmic circumstances, and they may be forced to separate.

This pattern of meeting up and then separating is one that is imprinted on both partners' subconscious, and if factors showing consistency, continuity, and permanence don't show up in a chart comparison, then this pattern will continue to repeat itself.

When these partners meet in this life, the encounter will be filled with excitement. The relationship may progress rapidly and become intimate quickly, and the partners may decide within a short time and to everyone's surprise to enter into a commitment. Then, as the relationship becomes routine, they may be disappointed. To maintain the "freshness" of the relationship, they may enter into a pattern of splitting up and getting back together, thus maintaining the initial excitement.

When these partners have become used to this pattern, they may accept it as their reality. If the relationship is important enough to them over time, then they must learn to maintain the delicate balance between independence and freedom on the one hand, and responsibility and commitment on the other hand.

NEPTUNE

Neptune represents sensitivity, receptive capacity, imagination, creativity, divine beauty, sympathy, idealism, affinity, and altruism. In addition, it represents faith, intuition, mysticism, spiritual awareness, and the capacity to achieve emotional and spiritual fulfillment. At its best, Neptune represents all that is supremely beautiful, lofty, and noble; yet when its manifestation in a chart is disharmonious, Neptune represents escape from reality, ambiguity, illusion, deception, and addictions. When its influence in a chart is strong, the person may wait for the ideal partner, then be disappointed when reality hits.

In karmic astrology, Neptune represents the soul's search for the spiritual ideal, and the purifying force that lifts us above the material world. Neptune also symbolizes the spirituality that opposes our animal instincts, or the sacrifice of desire that the soul must make in favor of the ideal, for only then can it reach the heights of consciousness.

The Neptunian yearning for unity with the cosmos can be achieved through holistic means such as yoga and meditation. A strong and harmonious Neptune in a chart can indicate that this individual is destined to be a spiritual teacher who can tune in to both the cosmic forces and to his or her higher self.

When Neptune in one chart influences a second chart, it shows a deep emotional connection and identification between the two people. They may even feel a total union between their souls.

On the downside, the blurring of boundaries between them can cause these two people to have a distorted view of reality. Their relationship may contain patterns of idealizing and illusion, particularly when Neptune forms disharmonious aspects. There may be a tendency to see the relationship through rose-colored glasses, or through a veil of illusion. When the veil is removed, there is likely to be deep disappointment and a fall from great heights.

The issue of projection is fundamental in all relationships in which Neptune is involved. The Neptune individual may project onto the partner his or her thoughts, responses, and feelings, as well as aspirations and unachieved goals. He or she may see the partner as an offshoot of him- or herself, and not as a separate entity. This may be true not only in a romantic relationship, but can manifest strongly in parent-child bonds as well.

The tendency of the Neptune individual to merge with the partner also gives birth to the desire to sacrifice oneself on the altar of the relationship, and when the partner fails to do likewise, the Neptune individual feels disappointed or even cheated.

The Neptune partner must take care not to see him- or herself as a victim or martyr, and absorb the fact that this illusion is created not by the partner, but rather is rooted in his or her own version of reality, which has led in fact to self-deception.

Neptune's harmonious aspects show a loving relationship, even telepathic in nature, which encompasses the emotional and spiritual needs of both partners. In this case, the Neptune person is willing to sacrifice for the partner, but without expectation of anything in return. This willingness to sacrifice stems from a karmic debt that the partner subconsciously knows must be paid off. This subconscious imprint causes the person to behave supportively and generously, with forgiveness and tolerance toward the other, being motivated by an inner sense that the partner behaved thusly toward him or her in a past life.

The Neptunian yearning to rise above reality can manifest as unconditional love. Such love is not dependent on receiving, and does not expect anything in return. Therefore, no disappointment can result, but rather only gratitude and elation.

PLUTO

Pluto, a planet associated with extremes, can manifest very negatively or very positively. Pluto represents extreme attitudes, behaviors, and feelings, as well as the extremes of life: death and rebirth. Pluto is also associated with the hidden corners of the soul, yet also with the heights of sensitivity and spirituality, and with rising above the limitations of the physical world. In the encounter with Pluto's planetary energies, a person influenced by its power faces existential choices between good and evil, light and darkness.

Only when we release our consciousness from the effects of negative energies can we open ourselves to higher positive energies. To do this, we must understand our deepest fears and their origins, and therefore we must be able to see clearly the psychological patterns that lie at the foundation of our behaviors.

Pluto represents the forces of both destruction and restoration. Its role is to destroy and to banish old psychological patterns and behaviors imprinted on the subconscious, both earlier in this life and in previous lives, which are now manifested as complexes. These negative patterns affect our everyday lives in the form of latent emotions that operate beneath the surface and that act as obstacles in our paths.

Pluto's activity pulls these emotions out of their latent state toward the surface, acting as a purifying force that can be accompanied by trauma. Yet banishing past patterns without taking into consideration the pain entailed in the process can bring about huge changes both in the individual and in humanity as a whole.

Pluto is the Great Transformer, and therefore associated with self-examination, taking us into the depths of ourselves and leading to raised consciousness and change through such processes as psychological treatment, psychoanalysis, or past-life regression therapy, which is healing through the release of negative subconscious content by returning to past lives.

Because Pluto's path is descent for the purpose of ascent, a person influenced by Pluto and driven by ego may express mainly the lowest sides of his or her personality. Only the person who makes correct use of Plutonian powers for ridding oneself of the "waste products" of past incarnations can rise above the surface and truly "take flight."

Pluto has magnetic intensity, and its influence can indicate a relationship involving power struggles. When Pluto's influence is positive, the two partners thrive on confrontation, yet its negative influence indicates a problematic relationship from which it is difficult to break free. If the Pluto partner is immature or not strong enough, the relationship can be destructive.

When Pluto exerts a strong influence on the partner's chart, it may be testimony to a symbiotic and even obsessive relationship. The clinging of the two partners has developed over several incarnations, wherein the partner has become dependent upon the Pluto individual. This pattern continues to manifest in this incarnation.

When Pluto's influence is negative, the Pluto person may substitute material goods for love, or manipulate in other ways in order to exert control. It is difficult indeed to leave a relationship in which Pluto is involved, because its influence is magnetic, binding the two partners inextricably. Even when they try to extricate themselves, the emotional effect remains. Therefore, it is up to the Pluto individual to finally break free of the "dense underbrush" of such a relationship, particularly from its emotional and psychological grip. As soon as the Pluto person lets go of the need to control, he or she frees up the energies needed to see the partner as an entity entitled to his or her own selfhood.

Pluto encourages an awareness process at whose culmination the person influenced by it learns to see him- or herself as in a newly polished mirror; he or she can also do this for the partner. When the person finally frees him- or herself of the fiery furnace of

Pluto's influence, he or she realizes that the true essence of love is the liberation of the loved one.

The ultimate achievement for the Pluto-influenced individual is knowing how to do this in the relationship itself. Through Plutonian intensity, both partners can reach shared insight and spiritual growth, exerting the inner forces that they have acquired to change not only their relationship but also their environment.

CHAPTER five

A WHEEL FOR TWO

Entwined in hidden cords
Tangled together
Warp and weft
Weft and warp
We are woven and untied
In the rhythm of our cycles of lives

—RUTH AHARONI

From the karmic astrology viewpoint, the birth chart in all its factors and components symbolizes the entirety of a person's life; it is actually a picture of the karma of a soul. The chart shows the positive and negative karma accumulated by the individual in all of his or her incarnations, and marks a direction according to which the person can balance his or her karma. The chart also shows how the person can fulfill the destiny chosen by his or her soul. Because every soul chooses for itself a unique path, every birth chart is unique.

When we want to find out whether two people have a karmic connection, we compare their birth charts to see if there is a karmic relationship and, if so, the nature of that relationship. Chart comparison enables understanding of karmic lessons that need to be learned through our relationships.

Chart comparison is fascinating and complex. To understand fully the relationship between two people, we must first understand the personal chart of each of the people involved. Only when we understand their individual charts can we try to understand the meaning of their combined charts.

Understanding the entire karmic constellation that brought these two people together in this life, whether long or short term, is in itself not a simple task, and it is always possible to investigate and discover more. However, a few simple methods can enable us to access this fascinating world, shedding a great deal of light on the subject. Some of these methods are presented in this chapter and throughout the book.

One method is the natural wheel technique, which, despite its generality, can be an inexhaustible source of information about an individual and his or her relationship with those around him or her. This method is good for those who do not know how to perform astrological calculations, or when the exact time of a person's birth is unknown. I will demonstrate the natural wheel method using the charts of Edgar Cayce and his wife, Gertrude.

Edgar Cayce, who was born in Kentucky on March 18, 1877, and died in 1945, was the prophet of the modern age. He became known as the Sleeping Prophet due to his psychic readings, which he performed while in a trance state. Throughout his life, Cayce gave thousands of readings on various subjects to people who sought his advice.

He became famous for his health readings, and despite not having had any medical training, he was able to diagnose illnesses and offer treatment advice based on what we now call holistic medicine. Among the many subjects that Cayce related to was astrology, reincarnation, and cosmic coupling.

Gertrude Evans was born on February 22, 1880, in Hopkinsville, Kentucky, where her family and Cayce's were neighbors. The two fell in love and married when they were in their twenties. Gertrude stood by Edgar's side and was infinitely devoted to him, and both devoted their lives to humane causes. They shared a deep emotional connection that can be seen in their combined charts, and when Edgar died, the bonds of love apparently pulled Gertrude to him, as she died three months later.

Let's now turn to the astrological constellation of Edgar and Gertrude Cayce.

The wheel of an astrological chart is divided into twelve segments called *houses*. In a chart calculated according to the exact time of a person's birth, the first house opens at a certain degree in one of the twelve signs. The sign in which the chart opens is called the *ascending sign*. However, in a natural wheel chart, the first house always opens at 0° Aries, and the other signs, in turn, open the rest of the houses at 0°, as we see in the figure 2.

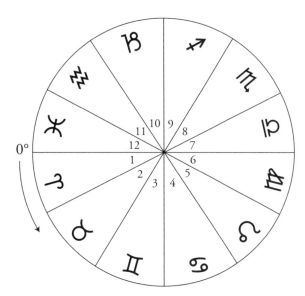

Figure 2—The Natural Wheel

To locate the position of the planets on a certain day, we use an *ephemeris* (planetary position tables) or astrology software. Using the ephemeris, we see that each of the planets is placed in a certain sign. Since every sign in the chart occupies 30°, each planet lies at a certain degree in a given sign.

The ephemeris also shows the location of the Moon's North Node, or *Dragon's Head*; the Moon's South Node, or *Dragon's Tail*, is located at the exact same degree of the opposing sign. The nodal axis, at the ends of which lie the Dragon's Head and Tail, represents the transition of the soul from its karmic past to the possibilities of its future karma. The key principle of the nodal axis can be summed up in the saying "Know from whence thou comest, and whence you go."

In this chapter, we'll relate to the Dragon's Head and Tail only on a technical level. Detailed information and background on the Dragon in the signs, houses, and relationships can be found in chapters 9 and 10.

Let's turn to the ephemeris and copy from it the locations of the planets as they appear in the birth dates of Edgar and Gertrude Cayce (a table showing the symbols representing the signs and the planets is at the end of chapter 3).

	☉	☽	☿	♀	♂	♃	♄	♅	♆	♇	☊
Edgar	28°23' ♓	12°12' ♉	11°42' ♓	15°43' ♓	11°13' ♑	2°03' ♑	12°49' ♓	21°16' ♌	3°39' ♉	22°56' ♉	9°54' ♓
Gertrude	3°22' ♓	21°51' ♋	9°57' ♓	27°35' ♑	3°50' ♊	20°17' ♓	13°16' ♈	7°07' ♍	9°35' ♉	25°29' ♉	13°12' ♑

Figure 3—Edgar and Gertrude Cayce's Astrological Data

We'll locate the planets in each wheel in the order of the signs (figures 4A and 4B):

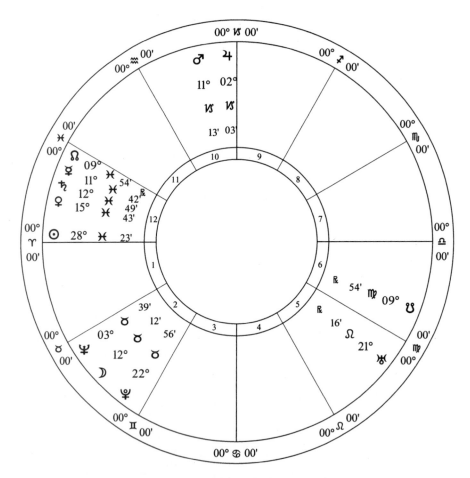

Figure 4A—The Natural Wheel for Edgar Cayce
March 18, 1877 / 3:00 p.m. Local Mean Time / Hopkinsville, Kentucky

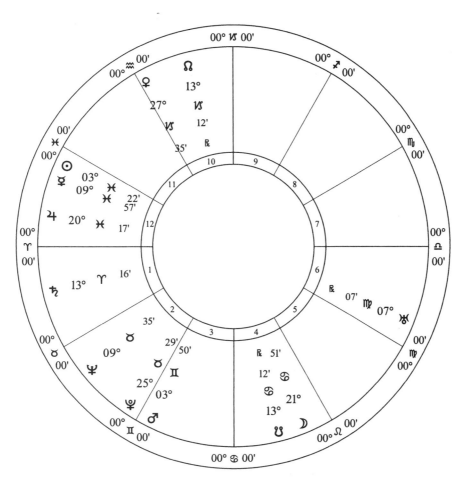

Figure 4B—The Natural Wheel for Gertrude Cayce
February 22, 1880 / 7:58 a.m. Local Mean Time / Hopkinsville, Kentucky

As we see, the planets lie at various distances from each other. The distances between planets are measured in degrees and are called *aspects*, or angles. The aspects, together with the rest of the factors in the chart, give us information about the karmic choice made by the soul.

When comparing two charts, the aspects formed between the planets in both charts show the relationship between these two individuals, and each type of aspect represents a different quality of relations.

For now, let's follow the *conjunction*, the most significant aspect in a karmic relationship. When the distance between two planets is 8° or less, they are *in conjunction*. For the moment, we are only relating to two planets in the same sign; thus, when planets occupy the same sign within a *permitted orb*, they are considered *conjunct*. The permitted orb of a conjunction is up to 10° (an explanation of aspect orbs is given in appendix B).

Now let's turn to the double natural wheel, and we'll place the planets of each of the wheels according to the data in figure 3, which is interspersed in the chart shown in figure 5. We place the man's planets on the outer wheel and the woman's planets on the inner wheel. The following conjunctions appear in the double chart that we've drawn:

- In the second house, there is a conjunction in Taurus between Edgar's Neptune and the Moon and Gertrude's Neptune. In both charts, Pluto is also placed in Taurus.
- In the sixth house, the conjunction between Edgar's Dragon's Tail and Gertrude's Uranus is in Virgo.
- In the tenth house, the conjunction between Edgar's Mars and Gertrude's Dragon's Head is in Capricorn.
- Many conjunctions can be seen in the combined twelfth house in Pisces, the most mystical sign of the entire zodiac.

In their combined charts, we indeed see a strong emphasis on Pisces, and Taurus is also prominent. As we will see later on, Taurus has a strong need for the stability and loyalty of couplehood, and its karmic purpose is for spiritual energy to transcend physical energy.

An emphasis on Pisces also shows that loyalty is an uppermost karmic goal. Edgar was particularly loyal, as even when he met his cosmic partner, he remained loyal to his life partner (a chart comparison of Edgar Cayce and Gladys Davis, his cosmic partner, appears in chapter 11).

An emphasis on Pisces in a couple's relationship also shows great spiritual potential and the possibility of transforming the relationship into an uplifting spiritual experience. Gertrude and Edgar Cayce enjoyed a relationship that was characterized by spirituality, both in a personal and a collectively human sense.

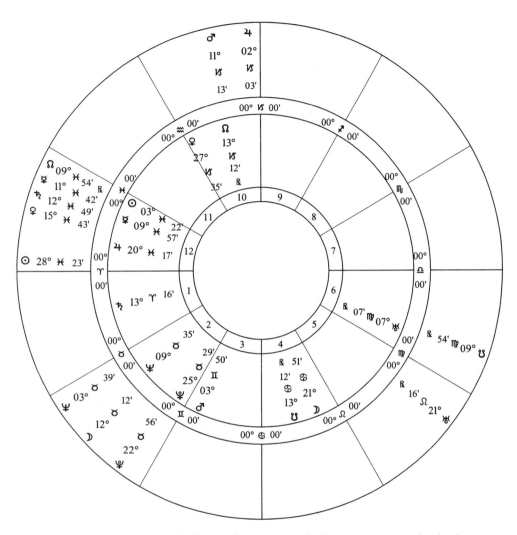

Figure 5—The Combined Charts of Gertrude and Edgar Cayce (Natural Wheels)

Inner Ring: Gertrude Cayce
February 22, 1880 / 7:58 a.m. Local Mean Time / Hopkinsville, Kentucky

Outer Ring: Edgar Cayce
March 18, 1877 / 3:00 p.m. Local Mean Time / Hopkinsville, Kentucky

In the following example we use the combined charts of Amir and Hila (figure 6), a couple whose karmic connection is manifested both in the chart and in their intense bond. Amir was born on July 30, 1946, and Hila was born on September 1, 1959. As we see, their combined charts show the following:

- Conjunctions in the fifth house in Leo.
- Conjunctions in the sixth house in Virgo.
- Another conjunction is seen in the seventh house in Libra between the Dragon's Head in Hila's chart and Neptune in Amir's chart.

In this chart comparison, we see that most of the planets are placed in Leo and Virgo, indicating a heavy energy load and resulting imbalance in the relationship that can be seen visually. The planetary energy is concentrated on one side of the chart, a situation that is difficult to sustain over time.

It so happens that Hila and Amir's relationship has been intense since the beginning. They fell in love immediately, and an obsessive emotional connection developed that led to a short marriage ending in an abrupt divorce.

Their relationship is a strong karmic connection between partners from the past that had to be consummated in this incarnation. However, an examination of the conjunctions shows that it also had to burn itself out quickly. Amir was swallowed up by Hila's excessively shed energy, and the relationship did not enable him to fulfill his individuality, which is particularly important to a Leo.

Hila overcame the emotional withholding typical of Virgo, and let Amir's Leo energies sweep her into the relationship; yet she quickly found herself on the giving side, with no one to "recharge her batteries." The way that she instinctively chose to save both herself and Amir was to forcibly cut the karmic cords that bound them, and leave him.

The next two chapters deal with profiling couplehood under the influence of the various signs, the karmic purpose of relationships with an emphasis on a specific sign, and the karmic significance of conjunctions in relationships.

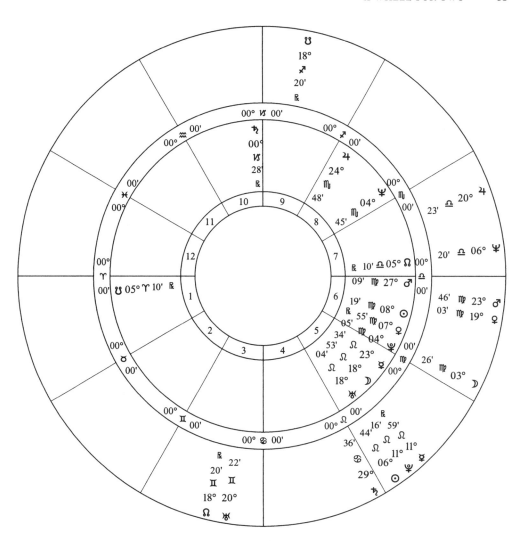

Figure 6—The Combined Charts of Hila and Amir (Natural Wheels)

Inner Ring: Hila

September 1, 1959 / 2:30 p.m. Standard Time / Time Zone: 2 hours East / Tel Aviv, Israel

Outer Ring: Amir

July 30, 1946 / 3:30 p.m. Standard Time / Time Zone: 2 hours East / Daylight Saving Time
/ Tel Aviv, Israel

CHAPTER SIX

I'LL FOLLOW YOU
THROUGH FIRE AND WATER

And this is the rule concerning the four elements:
Fire and earth are antagonistic, fire and air are compatible
Fire and water are antagonistic, earth and water are compatible
Earth and air are antagonistic, fire and fire are compatible . . .

—RABBI SAADIA GAON (10TH CENTURY)

If you're seeking an astrological answer to the most frequently asked existential question, "What is love?," then here's a simple answer: Love between two people is an attraction between their planets. Therefore, a relationship between two people is symbolized in astrology by the relationship between the planets in the two partners' respective charts.

Since the planets in a chart are located in various signs, and because the signs are divided according to the elements that make up the universe, Rabbi Saadia Gaon's saying, though simplistic, summarizes nicely the possible variations in the interaction between two people.

An attraction is common between two people whose signs are of the same element or between two people born under the same sign. Naturally, this initial attraction does not necessarily tell us about overall suitability or whether the relationship will be harmonious, but it underlines the oft-stated aphorism "Like seeks like." However, a relationship with an *emphasis* on a particular sign or element has karmic significance, and demands the learning of certain karmic lessons.

EMPHASIZED SIGNS IN A RELATIONSHIP

When at least three planets are posited within the same sign in a birth chart, that sign is considered *emphasized*. If the same sign is emphasized in one's partner's chart, then that sign's energy will have a strong effect on the relationship. The cluster of stars that is formed is called a *stellium*. An emphasized sign can manifest in either a positive or a negative way, depending on the nature of the *aspects* that the planets in the stellium form with other planets.

When a planet is at a distance of either 60° or 120° from another planet, the two planets form a *harmonious aspect*. When a planet is at a distance of 90° or 180° from another planet, the two planets form a *disharmonious aspect*. A detailed explanation of aspects can be found in appendix B.

The harmonious aspects between two charts show productive work that was already done in past incarnations, and the disharmonious aspects show problems in the relationship that the partners still need to work on and take the time to resolve in this incarnation.

Relationships in Aries

Relationships influenced by the sign of Aries are exciting, warm, and spontaneous. When the connection manifests in a positive way, the partners identify in each other their deepest inner needs and reflect them in one another, raising them to the surface. In this way they can confront these needs together and fill the voids constructively. These partners also encourage one another's assertiveness and courage to rise to challenges.

When the conjunction manifests in a negative way, the conflagration that is ignited is liable to burn up and consume the relationship. The partners are liable to react to each other with uncontrolled impulsiveness and outbursts of anger, to display controlling behavior, competitiveness, and a lack of consideration for one another. Each is likely to be focused on his or her own feelings, and to be unaware of hurting the other.

These partners will offend and take offense, will feel self-righteous, and their egos will not allow them to concede or see the justice in the other's side. Both are also liable to display inordinate independence, making it difficult for them to lead a shared, cooperative coexistence.

An emphasis on the sign of Aries in a relationship shows that each partner has come into the relationship in this incarnation in order to consolidate his or her identity. Both must develop their independence and individualism, together with self-restraint and maintaining balance. Thus, the disharmonious aspects activating the stellium will actually enable them to examine the common negative mechanisms at work in the relationship, because the negative trait is magnified in one's partner and the disharmonious aspects can act as catalysts for improvement.

Relationships in Taurus

Partners who establish a relationship under the influence of Taurus came into this life in order to fill physical and material voids accumulated over the course of various incarnations, and to extract bodily pleasure through occupying themselves with property, food, and sex. Taurus-emphasized relationships are based on the striving for material security and on the desire to live comfortably. Mutual feelings are strong and solid, and the romance between these partners is sensual and full of desire.

When this relationship manifests positively, Taurus-emphasized partners are courteous and patient with each other, and know how to pamper each other. However, because material and physical giving are an expression of love that the partners have for one another, when the stellium receives disharmonious aspects, the partners are liable to slip into materialism and animal sensuality. They must take care that their inordinate devotion does not turn into possessiveness and accompanying jealousy.

This couple's karmic purpose is to build devotion without possessiveness and to learn material giving that does not replace emotional giving. They must maintain stability, yet take care not to get stuck in a routine. They can keep things interesting by going out together, as they both value culture and the arts. Above all, they must refrain from getting carried away by carnal impulses, and learn to channel their physical love-energy into spiritual realms.

Relationships in Gemini

Gemini-emphasized relationships have more than two partners. Each of the partners brings into the relationship at least two personalities, and the couple dynamic actually becomes a group dynamic. This relationship will never be boring, because it is characterized by constant motion, both physical and mental. At the same time, this disquiet can be fatiguing, and the partners may annoy each other.

Harmonious relations in Gemini are based on a high mental level of understanding and adaptability between the partners, as well as problem-solving abilities and the solving of disputes using reason and mutual listening skills. Yet disharmonious aspects to this stellium can show that the relationship is superficial. This couple may not discuss important issues, or may bury them under mounds of meaningless chatter.

The avoidance of heavy issues is also a sign that in past incarnations the two did not develop emotional warmth, and did not learn to give of themselves totally. The curiosity prodding them to "taste" different types of relationships still arouses in them the desire to have relationships with others, naturally at the expense of their devotion to each other.

Geminis who see their personality traits reflected inordinately in their partners can be "shaken up" and motivated to think about making a change, prodding them to learn important karmic lessons of loyalty, trust, and stability.

Yet another critical karmic lesson for Geminis is learning to *feel* instead of *talk about feelings*. Though a difficult exercise for this couple, a "moratorium on words" is recommended, and will actually help them to properly process communication. When we silence our external words, our inner voice is released. In this way, the couple can progress toward their karmic goal, which is true communication in all its forms, in all realms of life.

Relationships in Cancer

Relationships influenced by Cancer are characterized by a high level of sensitivity and emotion. The partners in this relationship sense one another's feelings intuitively, and more than anyone else, can penetrate the shell under which the crab hides, responding with sensitivity to the other's distress. Both partners came into the relationship in order to realize and apply the value of family. They want to raise a large family in an exemplary home, and when the stellium creates a harmonious effect, they succeed at this endeavor, nurturing their nest with great attention and concern, and feathering it with love.

Cancers are natural caregivers, yet they are also capable of functioning as the ultimate dependent. When the relationship is imbalanced, this can manifest in a pervasive helplessness, or in a situation where one partner chooses to realize the true Cancer nature—bestowing warmth, protection, and shelter—and the other choosing to be the "child" in the relationship—dependent, demanding, and weepy. Disharmonious aspects of this stellium can display strong evidence of this phenomenon, when imbalance results from subconscious memories that affect the relationship.

If by chance one partner in this relationship lost a child in a past incarnation, and was born into this incarnation with a sense of bereavement, and the other partner lost a parent at an early age, leaving him or her with a fear of abandonment, then the two partners may form a symbiotic relationship, with one taking the role of parent and the other the role of child. In this case, the maternal energy does not allow separation, and the child energy does not seek autonomy.

Understanding the reasons for imbalance in such a relationship can be achieved through past-life regression therapy.

Relationships in Leo

Leo is the sign of love and romance, and partners with a Leo emphasis abound in emotional warmth, which they also externalize. Leo needs constant admiration, and when the relationship is positive, the partners, who are keenly aware of this mutual need, compliment one another and boost each other's egos. However, when disharmonious aspects are involved in this stellium, power struggles could occur, wherein each partner wants to be the sole controller, taking center stage and shoving the other aside lest he or she should usurp the other's "rightful place." In this case they may take turns being offended and feeling neglected, thereby harming the relationship.

An emphasis on Leo shows that the partners are compensating themselves for a simple life without glory and fame that they had in their past lives, or that they came into this incarnation in order to continue a life of abundance that was cut off prematurely. In this incarnation, they seek warmth and support, with both a homey environment and a glittery social life. This couple's home will be open, and they will constantly be hosting guests, whom the Leos think of as ornamentation for the house.

The karmic purpose of the Leo-influenced relationship is to give love abundantly, not only to one another but to anyone that they meet along the way. Leo energy inspires leadership powers, and the partners can be patrons, opening their home, their hearts, and their hands to those in need. Often Leos work for charitable causes or are patrons of the arts. Leos who harness themselves to tasks that contain a humanitarian element enrich their couplehood and fill it with inner satisfaction, a state that they could never achieve through activities whose sole objective is to demonstrate their external power, wealth, or brilliance.

Relationships in Virgo

Partners with an emphasis in Virgo have chosen to realize a relationship characterized by a high degree of mutual responsibility, as well as one in which candidness and honesty are keystones. Virgo seeks perfection in the other, and each partner in this relationship will pay attention to every detail and flaw in the other, yet their evaluation skills are at work from the relationship's outset, and Virgo does not indulge in illusions. The penetrating realism with which Virgos enter the world teaches them also to come to grips with reality and to rein in their tendency to criticize.

Virgo partners came into this life in order to fulfill obligations, both individual and social. They can blend their strengths to act and organize in an exemplary fashion to advance their objectives. However, because they are so industrious, they are liable to do their "homework" overefficiently and pedantically, stressing the practical and benefit-oriented side of life at the expense of pleasure.

In such a relationship, there is a danger of things becoming mechanical, with the partners relating to each other out of a sense of obligation instead of emotion. These partners need to learn to relax and take a time-out from the "musts" and "shoulds," finding the middle ground between obligation and emotion, and between discipline and spontaneity. It should be their mission to introduce a sense of lightness into both their relationship and outside relationships, thereby enabling all of their relationships to flow with more joy and sensitivity.

Relationships in Libra

A stellium in Libra that manifests positively shows that these two souls have learned in the past the art of compromise and harmony in couplehood, and they have come into this incarnation to experience couplehood at its best, having established honest and harmonious relations. These partners have the capability to experience love at its highest levels. They enjoy mutual consideration, and each is aware of the needs of the other and is willing to fulfill them.

A negative manifestation of a Libra-emphasized relationship will be felt if the desire to maintain peace at any price causes the partners to avoid dealing with problems that arise, instead sweeping them under the rug. The desire to remain calm and impartial can cause these partners to lose the spontaneity and the natural flow of the relationship, giving way to apathy or even coldness toward one another.

Furthermore, Libras have a tendency to pretend that "everything's okay," and avoid taking any action that requires them to grapple with flaws or to end the relationship. In this way, they prevent themselves from realizing the karmic purpose of their sign, which is to build a strong foundation for a healthy and fulfilling relationship.

It is therefore important that Libra partners learn to connect with their emotional selves without fear, because the fear of losing control and of strong emotions expressed prevents the release of pent-up anger. The desire to preserve a harmonious façade and to "do the right thing" extracts a heavy price: they actually sabotage the very internal harmony that is so important to them. Getting in touch with feelings and external expressions of frustration, anger, and even aggression will help these partners to cleanse from within, to regain balance, and to ultimately attain their longed-for harmony.

Relationships in Scorpio

A relationship with an emphasis in Scorpio is emotionally intense. The planets in Scorpio magnetize each other, the relationship is stormy, and the partners may experience extremes of love and hate. When the stellium forms disharmonious aspects, the relationship can be suffocating, making it hard for the partners to coexist, yet hard for them to part ways. These partners may tend toward coerciveness, suspicion, and jealousy toward one another. Scorpios are possessive not only regarding their present partners but also their past partners.

Partners who form a relationship under the influence of Scorpio are liable to burn each other out on karma-related conflicts regarding the acquisition of material goods or obsessive sexual behavior. They may waste energy on confrontations, or even on thoughts of revenge, thereby weakening their inner capacities and sabotaging their spiritual development.

Like their opposite sign, Taurus, Scorpios value loyalty, and for them, loyalty is manifested to an extreme. Therefore, it is important that in this incarnation both these partners give themselves permission to trust one another and neutralize their jealousy and possessive tendencies.

Self-awareness learning that includes relaxation and the controlled evocation of energies from low energy centers to high centers will help these partners to liberate themselves from extreme patterns that manifest in various realms of their lives. In the case of Scorpios, the ideal way to achieve spirituality and mystic unity is actually through the sexual experience.

Relationships in Sagittarius

Partners in a Sagittarius-emphasized relationship have perfected the art of freedom in their past lives, and in this life they are not willing to give up on it. Both these partners need their space, and if there are no negative aspects influencing the stellium, then each respects the other's emotional as well as physical space. This relationship is open and candid, with both partners revealing their feelings. They are kindhearted with each other, and there is a palpable sense of sharing and joy. Many matters, including the weightier ones, add interest to this partnership. There is no danger of routine prevailing in this relationship.

A preponderance of factors in the sign of Sagittarius can cause the relationship to "bubble over," so that the desire to neutralize the "fizz" and the attempt to find mental peace can take the partners out of the relationship: One or both partners may want to try physical or emotional adventures that distance him or her from the other partner.

Alternatively, the partners in this relationship could decide to have an open marriage, yet if the stellium is influenced by disharmonious aspects, then alienation could set in that may ultimately cause them to part ways. They must both understand that running away physically and disengaging mentally are not solutions, but are rather ways of ignoring reality, and these behaviors cannot continue long term.

A couple with a significant Sagittarius influence must always remember to value their good fortune; they must not sabotage it by excessive yearnings for freedom and adventure. Instead, they must work on nurturing the relationship under its own expansive canopy.

Relationships in Capricorn

Relationships with an emphasis on Capricorn have an air of seriousness and gravity about them. The partners are not swept up in emotions; they are realists, and don't harbor illusions, fancies, or caprices. They know what they want from one another and from the relationship. Life in this relationship goes according to known patterns, with few highs and lows; no one is looking for surprises. Romance is not a goal. This couple's karmic goal is to establish mature and stable relations wherein lie loyalty, honesty, and mutual responsibility.

When the stellium in Capricorn forms harmonious aspects, this relationship is like a good wine that improves with time. Over time, the sense of security and stability enables the emotional connection to grow. Thus, these partners can give themselves permission to soften and even show each other fondness.

However, if the stellium forms disharmonious aspects, then the rational, cold, calculating nature of the Capricorn relationship is liable to rule. The partners will only be interested in a goal orientation in which economic interests are prominent. Over several incarnations, the partners have grown accustomed to making do with little both emotionally and materially. Emotional scars sustained in the past have left them very guarded. Therefore, they have come into this life intending to build a relationship based on common practical interests, and not on emotions.

Such a relationship may only reinforce the partners' sense of gravity and emotional coldness. Therefore, these partners must make an effort to overcome their fears and open their hearts gradually to emotional warmth, so that their previous behavior patterns of inflexibility and self-defeat can be reversed.

Relationships in Aquarius

Partners influenced by Aquarius do not display their feelings publicly, yet they can be quite romantic within the privacy of the relationship. They don't feel obligated to express emotion, because they understand one another intuitively. They came into this incarnation to realize a relationship in which each of them respects the other's individual freedom and individuality.

When the Aquarian relationship is harmonious, there is unity of thought between the partners, yet even when they do not agree, they respect the other's opinion, unconventional though it may be. Partners influenced by Aquarius may even decide to live separately, yet maintain loyalty and a loving connection, because the separation actually stimulates them to want to spend time together. They may also decide, even at an early stage of the relationship, not to have sex, and to make do with a close mental connection.

Disharmonious aspects to this stellium may indicate emotional disengagement between partners. They will harness themselves to their own tasks, ideas, and circles of friends, and will carry on *alongside* each other, but not *with* each other.

Couples influenced by Aquarian energies must learn to commit themselves to the relationship just as they commit to their other tasks. Likewise, they must learn to connect to their emotional natures while maintaining the balance between their independence and their capacity to be involved emotionally.

Relationships in Pisces

When the aspects in a Pisces-emphasized relationship are harmonious, the relationship is delicate and romantic. The partners are very sensitive to one another, each picking up on the emotions of the other, paying attention to one another's emotional needs, each giving in to the other when necessary. Loyalty is an important value for these partners, as the sense of belonging causes Pisceans to feel anchored; otherwise the partners feel that they have lost their identities. When the relationship is unstable, each partner's situation is liable to be undermined. Therefore the stability of the relationship is critical.

Disharmonious aspects of this stellium can manifest as overdependency. The emotional involvement between Pisces partners can be destructive, causing them to move into a symbiosis in which neither partner lives an independent existence, but rather they function as a unit with two heads.

Pisceans have a tendency to feel like victims, and these partners are liable to play out the roles of tortured martyr and savior, even switching roles. Occasionally the tendency toward escapism can rule, with its own manifestations, such as alcohol or drug abuse.

These partners may also dabble together in mysticism, yet in an excessive way. Because the emphasis on Pisces arouses shared memories from past incarnations for these partners, it is important for them to know how to use this knowledge constructively to further their emotional development and spirituality.

These partners' channeling abilities can enable them to penetrate hidden layers of reality, and one of the karmic purposes in this shared incarnation is to develop a sense of proportion, lest they lose their orientation. At its best, this relationship enables the partners to develop together spiritually and to transform their couplehood to an emotionally and spiritually uplifting experience.

RELATIONSHIPS AND THE ELEMENTS

When there is an emphasis on a certain sign in both partners' charts, then the two partners are very similar and the match approaches that of twinship. Likewise, an emphasis on a certain element in both partners' charts reveals similarity and synchrony.

Astrology divides the twelve signs into four elements, so that each element includes three signs. These four groups are called *triplicities*. This division is based on an ancient division of the elements that make up the universe. Carl Jung applied this division in his psychological methods, linking the elements to the functioning of the consciousness.

♈ ♌ ♐ The element of fire is identified with **intuition.**

♉ ♍ ♑ The element of earth is identified with the **senses.**

♊ ♎ ♒ The element of air is identified with **thought.**

♋ ♏ ♓ The element of water is identified with **feelings.**

Deriving from this division are four personality traits:

The Fire Signs: Aries, Leo, Sagittarius

Those born under these signs are intuitive, temperamental, energetic, spontaneous, and extroverted. They radiate candor, enthusiasm, and self-confidence. They need lots of space, and it is important to them to stand out and demonstrate their individuality.

The Earth Signs: Taurus, Virgo, Capricorn

People born under these signs are sensuous and need contact with objects and material security. They are earthy, materialistic, practical, efficient, and organized. They excel in perseverance, deliberateness, patience, stability, and responsibility.

The Air Signs: Gemini, Libra, Aquarius

People born under these signs are mentally agile, quick learners, and excel at abstract thinking. They use logic and emotional restraint. They are friendly and communicative, and need constant mental and physical activity.

The Water Signs: Cancer, Scorpio, Pisces

People born under these signs are particularly sensitive, both inside and in their capacity to empathize with others. They have a rich imagination, a highly developed inner world, and a tendency to withdraw from reality.

People born under signs of the same element are matched, and are therefore attracted to one another. The fire signs match the air signs, and the earth signs match the water signs. A look at nature explains why:

- Fire and air go together because fire needs air in order to combust.
- Earth and water go together because water quenches the earth's thirst, and the earth stabilizes water.

In contrast:

- Water and earth both extinguish fire.
- Fire scorches the earth and boils water.
- Air and water create tempests.
- Air and earth create sand and dust storms.

Yet these statements are liable to be interpreted simplistically. It must therefore be emphasized that the suitability of two partners or the lack thereof must be related to not only the signs in which the partners' Suns are located, but also the signs in which the partners' Moons, ascending signs, and the signs of the other significators are located on their respective charts.

Optimally, each individual will be balanced regarding the elements, and the planets and the Ascendants will be split evenly between elements. Moreover, the blending of elements between both partners will be balanced. However, such a situation is uncommon. Often there is an emphasis on a certain element and a corresponding lack of another element, and many times people subconsciously choose partners in whom an element is prominent that is lacking in themselves. In other words, balance can be achieved through the partner.

A balanced division of elements enables a balanced experiencing of all aspects of our lives. An emphasis on a certain element in a person's chart is significant, and shows that in a past life his or her soul did not manage to achieve gratification in the realm represented by that element, and in this life the person feels a need to experience the aspects of life that are embodied in this element.

- When, in comparing charts, *fire* is prominent, the shared desire of both partners is to go through this incarnation living a spontaneous life brimming with experiences and adventures. There is a yearning to remove the boundaries and barriers of the past, and the partners place an emphasis on intense activity and thrill-seeking.

- When a comparison of charts shows an emphasis on *earth*, both partners will have a need for consolidation, material security, and a solid and organized life in the present incarnation. There is a mutual desire to overcome rash behavior, irresponsibility, withdrawing from reality, and past lives characterized by a lack of emotional or material stability.

- When *air* is prominent when comparing two charts, both partners strive for extensive and varied communication in this life, in an attempt to balance past lives in which the partners may have experienced loneliness, either voluntary or forced. The partners' sharing in this life is based on a need for mental stimulation, but at the same time there is a strong desire on both parts to maintain emotional and mental space.

- When, in comparing two charts, an emphasis on *water* appears, the partners' shared need in this life is to live their emotions to the fullest and to undergo deep emotional experiences in an intensive and total way. This desire acts to restore and correct past lives characterized by refraining from emotional experiences. Karmic balance for these partners will be achieved through the two-way flow of giving and receiving.

Suitability or a lack thereof between partners also manifests in aspects between signs:

- Signs of the same element are at a distance of 120° from each other. This distance is considered harmonious, and is known as a *trine* (see figure 7).

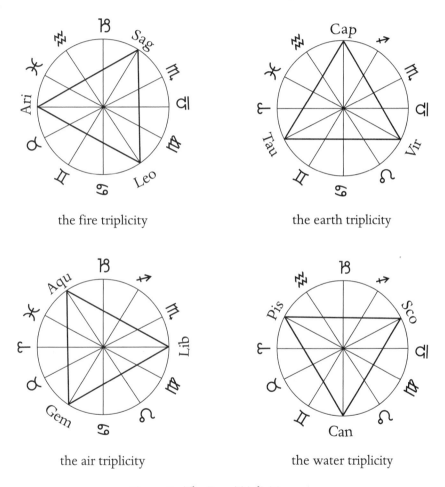

the fire triplicity

the earth triplicity

the air triplicity

the water triplicity

Figure 7—The Four Triplicities

- Fire and air signs are at a distance of 60° from each other. This distance is also considered harmonious, and is known as a *sextile*. The earth and water signs are also sextile to each other.

- In contrast, the fire and air signs are at a disharmonious aspect with the earth and water signs, as the distance between them is 90°. This aspect is known as a *square*.

Let's take another look at the combined charts, or *synastry*, of Edgar Cayce and his wife, Gertrude, shown in figure 5 on page 59. Water and earth are emphasized in their combined charts. Of the twenty-four factors in their chart, calculated based on the natural wheel technique, ten are in a water sign and eleven are in earth, showing extraordinary harmony between these two partners. The energy flow between them stands out even more because their respective charts produce several Grand Trines between planets in the earth element:

His Jupiter and Mars are in Capricorn

Her Venus and Dragon's Head are in Capricorn

His Dragon's Tail is in Virgo His Neptune and Moon are in Taurus

Her Uranus is in Virgo Her Neptune is in Taurus

A Grand Trine appearing in an individual's chart or two people's combined charts indicates a free flow of energy that enables the exploitation of skills acquired in past incarnations, and karmic lessons easily learned. For this application to be effective, it is best that the planets forming the trine also form some dynamic aspect with the other planets in the chart.

QUALITIES IN RELATIONSHIPS

Dividing the signs into three qualities, or *quadruplicities*, is another way to discover suitability between partners. Signs belonging to the same quadruplicity share related traits as follows:

- The *cardinal* signs—Aries, Cancer, Libra, and Capricorn—are initiators, go-getters, and goal-oriented types who love a challenge.

- The *fixed* signs—Taurus, Leo, Scorpio, and Aquarius—are stable, constant, and stick with a task until it is finished.

- The *mutable* signs—Gemini, Virgo, Sagittarius, and Pisces—love motion and change, and are curious and adaptable.

Further:

- When, in comparing charts, we find an emphasis on *cardinal* signs, the relationship is dynamic, challenging, and interesting. The relationship could be a reuniting of two people who were meant to be together in order to finish shared tasks that they began in a past life, or an encounter for the purpose of sharing creativity and new initiatives.

- A relationship characterized by an emphasis on *fixed* signs is a difficult one, because those born under fixed signs have a difficult time adapting and changing routines, habits, and thought patterns. This relationship has roots in previous incarnations, and the karmic attraction brings many conflicts to the surface. Facing the difficulties without faltering and coping with them wisely will enable *tikun*, balance, and over-coming karma.

- An emphasis on *mutable* signs shows a desire to adapt to the other partner and learn from one another. This relationship creates an opportunity for efficient exchange of information. The encounter between these partners helps each of them to extract knowledge acquired in past incarnations from the depths of the unconscious, and bring it to the surface.

Looking again at the Cayces' charts, we see that the mutable quadruplicity stands out. Of twenty-four factors in their combined charts, eleven, or half of the planets, are placed in mutable signs. There can be no doubt that this partnership helped Edgar Cayce not only to enter the unconscious realm and convey knowledge to his intimates and his clients, but also to get in touch with his psychic abilities and to channel esoteric knowledge that has been available to us since ancient times.

The Configuration of the Grand Cross
Aspects formed between signs in a quadruplicity are *squares* (90°) or *oppositions* (180°), so that any signs in a quadruplicity form a *Grand Cross*.

A Grand Cross has strong karmic significance, and its appearance in an individual's chart or in a couple's combined charts shows the imprint of a special fate in their lives. The cross shows that the soul chose to grapple in this life with problematic karmic patterns imprisoned in the subconsciousness, which waited for the opportune moment in order to get resolved. The affected person's struggle to liberate him- or herself from the karma-blocking bonds is liable to manifest in difficult life circumstances.

The most difficult square relationship is, as we noted, a relationship between fixed signs. Yet despite the difficulty, or even because of it, the relationship will have an element of challenge to overcome this difficult karma, and hidden therein are many opportunities to learn, engage in *tikun*, and elevate spiritually.

The fixed signs are spokes on the zodiac, and it is no coincidence that the fixed signs appear in Ezekiel's vision of the chariot in Ezekiel 1:10: "As for the likeness of their faces, they had the face of a man; and they four had the face of a lion on the right side; and they four had the face of an ox on the left side; they four had also the face of an eagle." (In Ezekiel's vision, the eagle astrologically represents Scorpio, and the human represents Aquarius, the only human fixed sign.)

Figure 8—The Fixed Grand Cross

CHAPTER SEVEN

TWO BY TWO

The present rolls back into the past
Soul fastens to soul
They are born and reborn again and again
To retrace the tightrope of life.

—RUTH AHARONI

T he conjunction, the strongest aspect appearing in a chart, brings together two or more planets whose shared energy has a much stronger effect than that of any other aspect. A conjunction of three or more planets is called a *stellium*, and it focuses our attention on the karmic role of the sign in which it occurs.

When comparing two charts, conjunctions between personal planets show a similarity between the two individuals, yet in and of themselves they do not indicate a relationship spanning incarnations. A conjunction between personal planets takes on karmic significance only if it also forms some aspect with karmic planets.

Conjunctions between karmic and personal planets show that there were shared activities and events in the past lives of these two souls. Many conjunctions show that they met in several past incarnations, and that their encounter in this life is meant to urge their souls to balance and repair the karma shared by them.

A conjunction is either harmonious or disharmonious, depending on the aspects that it forms with other planets from both charts. When the planets in a conjunction form harmonious aspects with other planets, then the conjunction is manifested positively; conversely, when the planet in the conjunction forms disharmonious aspects, then the facet of the relationship represented by the conjunction will be fraught with a degree of difficulty of one type or another.

Every conjunction offers a clue to the possible nature of the relationship between the two souls in the past, and shows the imprint left on the soul lives of the individuals and on the present patterns of their relationship. Following is an overview of conjunctions between two charts and their interpretations.

SUN-SUN

This aspect shows warmth and closeness between the two individuals, who have a strong effect on one another. They understand one another, and even if there is an age gap, they both function at the same level of maturity.

If the Suns also form aspects with karmic planets that show a relationship that spans incarnations, then these two shared a past life in which they were equals; possibly they were the same gender. They may compete, but there is an underlying current of mutual respect.

Competition between these two may bring out the best in them, stimulating the creative urge. Yet it is likely that each of them aspires to be the star of the show, possibly resulting in power struggles. The likelihood of this all depends upon the sign in which the Suns are located, and the other aspects that the Suns form.

As we have seen, in Leo, for example, power struggles can be prominent, because each individual wants to play the starring role. Aquarians, on the other hand, usually respect others' space and "act" on two separate stages. And Libras, with their capacity for giving in and compromise, tend to soften the friction, enabling cooperation and harmony.

SUN-MOON

The Sun, which represents the active, male essence, supports the action of the Moon, which represents the passive and receptive female essence. The Sun individual has a strong effect on the Moon individual, elucidating and arousing in the Moon individual emotional patterns from a past incarnation.

The emotional ties between these two are strong, including physical attraction, which will be manifested only if a sexual relationship is an option. There is deep understanding here, and the relationship is basically harmonious, if it is not flawed by many negative aspects.

When this aspect is formed between two individuals, and the Sun in the woman's chart is in conjunction with the Moon in the man's, it indicates that it is she who "wears the pants" in the relationship. This conjunction, if reinforced by karmic planets, can indicate the continuation of a fertile cooperation and warm friendship from a past incarnation, including the possibility of a mother-son or father-daughter relationship between the two in a past incarnation. This aspect often appears in the combined charts of cosmic individuals.

SUN-MERCURY

In this conjunction, the Sun individual can activate the Mercury individual's mental powers and influence his or her opinions, while the Mercury individual's ideas inspire the Sun individual, activating his or her creativity and powers of expression. Both share common areas of interest and effective communication, and understand each other well.

If this conjunction forms aspects with karmic planets, it may indicate that in a past incarnation these two shared a teacher-pupil relationship, and the Sun individual acted as the authoritative figure that contributed the support, knowledge, and advice.

SUN-VENUS

At its best, this is an aspect of sympathy, friendship, cooperation, consideration, admiration, and magnetic attraction. These two individuals are fond of one another and enjoy each other's company. If the planets involved in the conjunction also form harmonious aspects with karmic planets, then these two are enjoying the continuation of a positive friendship, romance, or business relationship from a past incarnation.

A disharmonious manifestation can indicate domination on the part of the Sun individual, who takes on the role of patron of the Venus individual as a result of an unequal relationship between them in a past incarnation.

SUN-MARS

This aspect indicates an intense unity of energies that can lead both individuals to accomplish impressive achievements that are a continuation of their activity in a past existence, if karmic planets are involved. These two must each respect the will of the other, as well as each other's independence; otherwise, power struggles will mark the relationship.

This aspect can also indicate that these two had a boss-subordinate relationship in the past, whether in a military context or while working to accomplish a task that required sustained effort in order to reach a shared goal that was in some way groundbreaking.

In a romantic relationship, this aspect may indicate a strong physical attraction. In any case, both individuals are active and take initiative in this area, as in both individuals, male behavior patterns are imprinted from a past incarnation.

SUN-JUPITER

This aspect has an abundance of energy that can be exploited productively or wasted, depending upon the entirety of the two charts involved. It also contains the potential for mutual spiritual growth: the Jupiter individual expands the horizons of the Sun individual, and the Sun individual ignites the superior ideas of the Jupiter individual, yielding a beneficial connection for both.

When this aspect also forms a harmonious connection with karmic planets, it shows that both have pleasant shared memories of a past incarnation, and that the former relationship between them thrived on joy and optimism. Often, these two souls shared ideological or religious fellowship in a past incarnation, and their renewed encounter in this life is a continuation of a vital and inspired cooperation.

SUN-SATURN

In this aspect, the karmic lesson of the Sun individual is to learn to be more mature, serious, and practical, to be more responsible and realistic, and to learn to exploit his or her power and skills effectively. The Saturn individual's task is to learn to be more self-confident, spontaneous, and vital.

The Saturn individual must learn to overcome his or her jealousy of the Sun individual, as well as to moderate the inclination to criticize and make demands of him or her, as these two tendencies are repressive to the Sun individual and dampen his or her enthusiasm.

This contact may indicate a past father-son relationship, and if the aspect is disharmonious, it is possible that the father in that relationship was a stern disciplinarian and forced the son to carry his burden. The father's attitude may have been rigid or cold, absent of any demonstrations of love or fondness. Now it is up to the Saturn individual to learn to be more open and warm.

When this conjunction is manifested positively, it is a stable aspect that ensures loyalty and a long-term connection.

SUN-URANUS

This contact is typified by a behavior pattern characterized by independence that was imprinted on the two souls in past incarnations. In this life, both individuals seek to continue guarding their uniqueness. This relationship is full of vitality, thrills, changes, and surprises, and there is a magnetic attraction and electricity between these two souls.

When this conjunction is influenced by harmonious aspects, the relationship is arousing and exciting, but when it is influenced by disharmonious aspects, it may be fraught with tempers, and the individuals may be forced to seek refuge with others.

SUN-NEPTUNE

The interpretation of this conjunction depends very much upon aspects that it forms with other planets. When this conjunction is manifested harmoniously, then the relationship is characterized by tenderness, sensitivity, empathy, understanding, and inspiration. Between these two there is an uplifting spiritual connection and a shared interest in either mysticism or art.

When this conjunction is disharmonious, the Neptune individual may mislead or delude the Sun individual, who may see the Neptune individual as a spiritual person who can lift him or her to the heights, when actually the Neptune individual is simply pretending to be spiritually motivated.

Yet another possible manifestation of a disharmonious conjunction is that both may be involved in cultlike activities, or together become addicted to drugs or alcohol.

SUN-PLUTO

This is an intense and dynamic aspect, in which two extremes—light and darkness—meet and are magnetically attracted. This encounter triggers subconscious memories from past incarnations—even ancient ones—enabling intensely thrilling and sensual experiences.

After the encounter between these two individuals—whether short or long term—both are changed forever.

A disharmonious manifestation of this aspect shows a power struggle and clashes of wills. Such a conjunction may cause to surface memories from a past incarnation in which each individual filled a central role in the same context, and in this life, each is still trying to control the other.

The karmic goal in this aspect is to teach the two to unite in a balanced fashion the energetic intensity created by the encounter of their two forces.

MOON-MOON

This aspect indicates a close connection between two people who pick up on each other's feelings and respond to one another's moods. They share an immediate, intuitive understanding and exert a mutual influence, both positive and negative.

If this conjunction forms an aspect with a karmic planet, it may indicate that these two have a similar family background, and if the aspect is harmonious, then in this incarnation the link between them enables them to re-create the same warm family unit to which they belonged in the past. If this conjunction forms a contact with a karmic planet connected to the fourth house, we see a clear karmic connection between relatives from the past.

MOON-MERCURY

This aspect shows a two-way flow of feelings and ideas between these two. The Moon individual senses the Mercury individual's ideas, and the Mercury individual understands the Moon individual's feelings. When this aspect is harmonious, there is a balanced merging of the Mercurial rational and the Lunar emotional orientations.

When this aspect is disharmonious, these two irk each other, and neither one can trust the emotional stability of the other. From a karmic standpoint, we have here a "rerun" of a caregiver-patient relationship from the past, and this aspect can arouse memories of childhood or youth from past incarnations.

MOON-VENUS

This aspect shows a particularly sensitive relationship between the two individuals. It has a touch of the female, which, if manifested harmoniously in a chart comparison of a couple, indicates a capacity on the part of the man to get in touch with his anima, or female side. This capacity enables the two to develop without barriers. They may pamper each other, giving each other love and emotional security. Even when this contact is not harmonious, there is still a strong emotional connection, yet jealousy and competitiveness may get in the way.

When this conjunction forms aspects from karmic planets, the relationship may arouse memories of previous emotional, familial, or romantic connections between the individuals.

MOON-MARS

This aspect expresses intense physical and emotional energy between the two, and the link between them raises to the surface strong emotional patterns, either positive or negative. This is a relationship marked by impulsiveness, that brings to the fore the instinctual side of both individuals. In a romantic relationship, this aspect expresses strong sensual energy and attraction.

If the Mars individual is a woman, it is almost certain that she is the initiator in this relationship. At its best, this is a refreshing partnership, full of vitality, in which both sides express their feelings spontaneously and without inhibition. In addition, the assertiveness and ambition of the Mars individual provides a safety net for the Moon individual.

If this aspect is manifested disharmoniously, and the Moon individual is needy and tries to coerce the Mars individual, then resentment may develop between the two. Moodiness and oversensitivity on the part of the Moon individual may irritate the Mars individual, who may behave belligerently, disturbing the emotional balance of the Moon individual.

In this aspect, the karmic lesson for the Mars individual is to learn to consider and cope with others' feelings, while the lesson for the Moon individual is to gather strength as well as to gather and focus his or her energies.

If the conjunction forms an aspect with karmic planets, and the relationship is that of mother-son or father-daughter, then there may be a hint of an Oedipus or Electra complex whose origins lie in a romantic relationship from the past. Because this aspect awakens memories of tight past relations between these two, its disharmonious manifestation may trigger in both either possessiveness or jealousy, binding them to each other in spite of themselves.

MOON-JUPITER

At its best, this aspect inspires mutual loyalty and security; these two nurture and protect each other. The contact enables the Moon individual to break free of the subconscious level and rise to the highest level of consciousness. The Jupiter individual can, by the same token, aid the Moon individual in breaking out of his or her shell and liberating him- or herself from inhibitions and repressive behavior, creating an atmosphere of openness and optimism.

If the Moon individual is passive and given to negative emotional patterns, then under the Jupiter individual's influence, he or she may begin to believe that good fortune is within reach, and permit him- or herself to feel abundance instead of the existential scrimping that may have become habitual.

When this conjunction forms aspects with karmic planets, it hints at a past familial relationship characterized by emotional and/or material support. Another possibility is a past relationship wherein the Jupiter individual took it upon him- or herself to support the Moon individual as a benefactor, and now the Moon individual is repaying the Jupiter individual.

MOON-SATURN

This is not an easy conjunction, because the demanding Saturn individual limits the Moon individual, forcing him or her to be self-sufficient, efficient, and effective. The Saturn individual's influence is both strong and irksome, and the Moon individual may feel smothered. This relationship is a weighty one, and in the case of a disharmonious contact, this conjunction may manifest materialistic tendencies alongside emotional coldness.

When the other factors in both charts show cooperation between these two, then this contact gives them a sense of security and protection. This relationship may hint at a parent-child relationship, or one in which both individuals co-parented in the same family, and they are now repeating the familial pattern, wherein the Moon individual takes the warm and protective mothering role, and the Saturn individual takes the commandeering, paternal role.

The present lesson for these two is to learn the right degree of control over emotions. The Saturn individual must learn to go with the emotional flow, and the Moon individual must learn to balance and stabilize his or her emotions.

MOON-URANUS

This contact shows immediate thrills and attraction between these two, yet the relationship is marked by emotional instability, disquiet, tempers, and sudden and unanticipated change. This conjunction can indicate a past relationship, whether as romantic partners, as residents of the same community, or as members of a commune. Whatever the relationship, it was cut off suddenly. In this incarnation, too, despite the fact that the Moon individual wants to domesticate the Uranus individual, this contact in and of itself does not guarantee a lasting connection.

The karmic role of the Uranus individual is to "break down the walls of the house" in which the Moon individual has taken refuge, forcing the latter to emerge from his or her fortress, and teaching him or her to cope with the storms in the outer world.

This aspect suggests a return of the Uranus individual to his or her past role as the Moon individual's leader, continuing in his or her efforts to draw the Moon individual out of his or her conformism and encouraging personal growth and spiritual development.

MOON-NEPTUNE

When this conjunction is harmonious, these two are exquisitely sensitive to each other, understanding each other's emotional needs. If the relationship is romantic, they are likely to designate their home as a gathering place for spiritual activity, or they may insulate themselves and hide from the world.

This contact shows a strong spiritual-emotional connection and a shared interest in mysticism that is a continuation of one shared in past incarnations. If other factors indicate such, this aspect can show that the Neptune individual acts as a spiritual guide to the Moon individual. If the conjunction is disharmonious, emotional problems and memories from events in past lives may flicker in the subconscious, constituting an obstacle in both their paths. Memories of deception and misleading from past incarnations may hover, in which the Moon individual was the Neptune individual's victim.

MOON-PLUTO

This contact shows an emotional connection whose roots lie deep in past incarnations of both souls. The contact is an intense one that causes the subconscious needs of each individual to rise to the surface, such that each can emerge from his or her emotional solitude and grow. The capacity of the Pluto individual to penetrate into the layers of the past and awaken buried memories can aid the Moon individual to change and undergo an emotional transformation. This is a magnetic connection that also incorporates a strong sensual attraction in the event that a sexual relationship is an option.

If this conjunction forms disharmonious aspects, then the Pluto individual's formidable power can subdue the Moon individual. In this case, the Pluto individual may trigger in the Moon individual an outburst of emotion or of negative memories. Such an emotional tidal wave may generate an internal storm in the Moon individual, making this contact possibly destructive to him or her.

MERCURY-MERCURY

In and of itself, this is not an emotional connection, but rather a mental one in which the two can freely express their ideas and feelings. They think alike, understand each other, and share a common language, even if they are inhibited with others. With each other, communication is fluent, and they are on the same wavelength.

When this conjunction is harmonious, it is almost certain that these two share a worldview, and even if there are gaps between their ideas, they bridge them with understanding and freely flowing communication.

If the conjunction forms disharmonious aspects, there could be competition between them, yet it will usually be of a healthy nature. It is also likely that they compete for verbal space, and if there are no aspects to neutralize the disharmony, then these two may wear each other out and seek a break from each other.

When this conjunction forms aspects with karmic planets, both sense that they already learned their shared domains of interest in the past, and they are now continuing to share these interests in the present. It is also likely that they lived in the same place in a past incarnation, or that they were relatives.

MERCURY-VENUS

This aspect expresses a comfort that expedites mental and emotional communication between these two. They enjoy sharing their thoughts and feelings as well as mutual empathy and a pleasant friendship.

When the conjunction forms aspects with karmic planets, it indicates that these two had a similar cultural background, which they are continuing today while engaging in mutual learning. The Mercury individual helps the Venus individual to understand feelings, and the Venus individual "civilizes" the Mercury individual and his or her mode of expression.

A good connection with the second, third, or fourth house can indicate past lives as family members from a high stratum of society.

MERCURY-MARS

This is an active and vital connection in which the Mars individual stimulates the intellect of the Mercury individual, and the Mercury individual in turn improves upon the Mars individual's ideas. The contact sharpens the rational side of both, and they compete well in a "battle of the minds."

In a harmonious aspect, this competition has a positive effect on the mental activity of both individuals, yet in a disharmonious aspect, there may be intellectual struggles, and both may be opinionated, inattentive, or dismissive of the other's ideas. There may also be a tendency toward a verbalization of sex on the part of the Mercury individual, and in a couples' relationship this could frustrate the Mars individual, as talking may substitute for doing.

If this conjunction obtains karmic aspects that connect it to the third house, it could be an indication of a sibling connection from the past. When the conjunction is disharmonious, fraternal conflict from the past is likely, which may have repercussions in the present, and which must be resolved.

MERCURY-JUPITER

This contact brings together the high level and the low level of consciousness. When the conjunction is manifested harmoniously, it indicates good communication between the two and a shared interest in many areas. The Mercury individual helps the Jupiter individual to bring his or her ideas to fruition, and the Jupiter individual in turn helps the Mercury individual to avoid getting bogged down in mundane details, and instead expand his or her consciousness.

When this conjunction is manifested disharmoniously, there could be hypocrisy, a lack of honesty, or an inconsistency of ideas in the relationship, as the Mercury individual may think the Jupiter individual pretentious, and the Jupiter individual may think the Mercury individual superficial.

A karmic connection between these two may indicate that the Mercury individual was the Jupiter individual's pupil in past incarnations. The relationship may have been that of disciple and spiritual guide, such as a rebbe or guru, but in any case, the Jupiter individual helped the Mercury individual to open new paths to consciousness, and the shared experience helped them both to develop both spiritually and mentally.

MERCURY-SATURN

This is an aspect that points to a serious and considered approach and a defined goal for the relationship. The Saturn individual teaches the Mercury individual a lesson in shouldering responsibility, aspiring to order and organization in their shared dealings. The Saturn individual pushes the Mercury individual toward achieving and shows him or her the means for acquiring wisdom. He or she acts as an example of maturity, in turn giving the Mercury individual a sense of security.

The Mercury individual is used to turning to the Saturn individual for encouragement and support, either material or emotional, having always felt protected in his or her presence, as this contact is a reenactment of either a parent-child or a teacher-pupil relationship in a past incarnation.

However, when this conjunction is disharmonious, the Mercury individual feels restricted and pressured by the Saturn individual's demands, and by the discipline that he or she imposes. The Mercury individual also feels that the Saturn individual's heavy style doesn't fit his or her youthful mentality, and that the Saturn individual thwarts his or her self-expression, as well as imposing too-high standards that, instead of helping the Mercury individual to progress, may paralyze him or her.

This aspect indicates the role of the Saturn individual as a stern father or educator from a past life, and both may consequently sense dissatisfaction and frustration in this relationship.

MERCURY-URANUS

This conjunction indicates a relationship wherein there is a dimension of openness and continual renewal, and which constitutes a mental and intellectual stimulus that expedites both individuals' awareness. The contact with the Uranus individual causes the rational Mercury individual to feel thrills, stimulating the creativity and inventiveness of both, as well as possibly teaching telepathic communication between them.

If there is reinforcement on the part of other factors, this aspect can indicate that in a past incarnation these two were involved in social action, and it is likely that they even were both members of some humanitarian organization. In this incarnation they have met up in order to reawaken their reformist ideas and bring them to fruition. A disharmonious conjunction may show that these two stimulate each other to the point of annoyance and disquiet, and their relationship will therefore show signs of instability.

MERCURY-NEPTUNE

This contact combines logic and sound judgment with inspiration and intuition. The Mercury individual contributes a dimension of mental capacity and practicality to the Neptune individual's sweeping vision. These two have a strong mental and emotional connection, and they perceive each other intuitively, without the need for superfluous talk.

The Neptune individual's karmic role is to stimulate the Mercury individual's mental powers and creativity, yet if the contact is disharmonious, the encounter may be illusory and can end in disappointment.

This aspect can indicate that the individuals belonged to an esoteric or secret society in a past incarnation. When the conjunction is harmonious, it may indicate that the Mercury individual received spiritual assistance from the Neptune individual; yet a disharmonious contact may indicate that the Neptune individual steered the Mercury individual wrong or deceived him or her.

MERCURY-PLUTO

This aspect shows a strong mental attraction. If the conjunction is harmonious, it is an excellent aspect for spiritual development because the Pluto individual does not make do with what meets the eye, but rather delves more deeply into things. The Mercury individual develops thinking ability, and is changed by his or her closeness to the Pluto individual. If there are other factors that reinforce this direction, then we may have a relationship between a pupil and a charismatic teacher from a past incarnation, and the Mercury individual continues to be pulled to follow in the footsteps of the dominant Pluto individual.

If the contact is disharmonious, the Pluto individual may try to force his or her will on the Mercury individual. Here, too, the Mercury individual may be attracted to the Pluto individual, who in a past incarnation exerted mental control over him or her, and therefore may forfeit his or her independence. If the Mercury individual nevertheless tries to express an opinion, the Pluto individual may react with an outburst, and if the Mercury individual is not strong enough to withstand it, he or she may fold in the face of the Pluto individual's anger.

VENUS-VENUS

This aspect is an excellent one for either a social or a business relationship, as it indicates agreement, empathy, understanding, and cooperation, as well as a similar outlook on love. Even the way that these two choose to spend their free time is similar. This aspect also indicates loyalty and deep feelings for each other, and the potential for a long-term relationship.

When this conjunction forms aspects with karmic planets, it indicates that in the past these two had shared interests. If it has a connection with the seventh house, it can hint at a marriage between these two in a past incarnation; if the connection is in the third or fourth house, it can indicate a past familial relationship. These two now continue to sense a familial connection, and if there are no significant disharmonious aspects, they will continue to enjoy the connection and the stimulation that it offers.

VENUS-MARS

This is a classic romantic aspect: the sexual urge of Mars connects with the fond love of Venus. When this combination obtains an aspect from any karmic planet, without a doubt we are looking at a love relationship from the past that has returned to the delight of the individuals involved.

Even if this relationship is same-sex in this incarnation, a karmic attraction is indicated between two people who enjoy each other's company, and the connection between them is dynamic and full of vitality and interest. When the conjunction is between Venus in the man's chart and Mars in the woman's, then the man has an opportunity to tune in to his anima, or inner female, and the woman likewise has an opportunity to identify with her animus, or male component. If no aspect contradicts it, this relationship will be heartfelt and open, and suited to doing business as well.

VENUS-JUPITER

This contact shows empathy, generosity, openness, and open-mindedness. In this relationship we see uninhibited love absent of all bonds and restrictions, and the relations are full of joie de vivre, optimism, and pleasure. When the conjunction has a disharmonious tint, we see an element of laziness and hedonism, wherein the two place an emphasis on pleasure and enjoyment.

When this conjunction has a karmic contact, then these two are continuing past relations in which the Jupiter individual was devoted to Venus, and has returned to add to the Venus individual's pleasure. This is a "bonus" for good karma whose harmonious aspects show that in a past incarnation, the Jupiter individual was the Venus individual's kindhearted patron.

If other factors indicate such, the Jupiter individual acted as a spiritual teacher or mentor to the Venus individual, and in this life, continues to inspire the Venus individual with his or her wisdom and encourage his or her unending search for knowledge. Together, they are continuing a relationship filled with spiritual inspiration and pleasure.

VENUS-SATURN

By itself, this aspect promises loyalty and stability in a relationship whose roots lie in past lives, and in which the Venus individual was sheltered and supported by the Saturn individual's protection.

When this conjunction is harmonious, the Venus individual willingly accepts the friendly authority of the Saturn individual and recompenses him or her with appreciation and love. However, when it is disharmonious, the sheltering may be irksome and cumbersome; the love that would otherwise flow is hampered by the sense that it is obligatory, and the weight of responsibility offsets the pleasure in the relationship. The Saturn individual may turn cold and irritable, and fail to respond to the Venus individual's emotions. Such a disharmonious conjunction can even be indicative of difficult memories from a past relationship that still trigger fear and suspicion that characterize the present relationship.

If the relationship in question is a romantic one in which the woman is represented by Venus and the man by Saturn, and the conjunction is linked to the third or fourth house, then it may indicate a father-daughter or little sister–big brother relationship from a past incarnation.

VENUS-URANUS

This contact indicates strong, immediate attraction and an exciting relationship that stimulates interest on both parts and is the renewal of a similar relationship in the incarnational past. This is an unconventional relationship that has not been steady.

If it is a romantic relationship, the two are magnetically attracted, and they sense that they are continuing an exciting acquaintanceship that began in the past. This aspect indicates emotional intensity, yet it is an intensity that cannot be sustained. The aspect itself may indicate instability, so that if no other factors indicate continuity, the relationship may end as suddenly as it began.

It is nearly certain that in its previous incarnation, this relationship ended without becoming permanent. If there are aspects that do indicate continuity, however, then this time there is a chance that the two will manage to build a solid foundation and retain the newness and excitement despite the relationship's having been "institutionalized."

When this conjunction obtains a disharmonious tint, despite the fact that while it is a stimulating aspect, it can also trigger nerves. The Uranus individual stimulates the natural love instinct of the Venus individual, but at the same time can arouse possessiveness that, if not reined in, may cause the Uranus individual to rebel under the repression. Therefore, the karmic lesson in the case of the Venus individual is to learn to give love that does not bind.

This is an aspect that can indicate a shared interest in New Age realms and a desire for spiritual growth.

VENUS-NEPTUNE

This contact has a poetic facet that indicates a soul connection of a two-way emotional flow, as well as telepathic understanding. The Neptune individual encourages the Venus individual to express a more spiritual love, and the Venus individual encourages the Neptune individual to express intuitions in a more down-to-earth fashion. The Neptune individual beckons the Venus individual with his or her charm, but if the conjunction obtains a negative manifestation, the charm could go to waste.

This encounter triggers memories of a past incarnation in which these two spent enchanted hours together. Even if, as a result of other aspects, the relationship in this life doesn't work out, and the initial magic turns out to be illusory, in the emotional realm, these two will always yearn for the dreamlike and romantic existence that the contact arouses in them.

VENUS-PLUTO

This conjunction indicates a strong karmic relationship and a deep emotional connection between the two souls. In a romantic relationship, this is manifested in a strong sensual attraction and desire. The Pluto individual has a magnetic effect that the Venus individual finds difficult to resist. When this aspect is manifested positively, the Pluto individual can affect the Venus individual in the direction of growth and self-discovery on all levels.

If this conjunction is disharmonious, the Pluto individual may employ dominant or manipulative tactics on the Venus individual, and the relationship may be coercive and typified by jealousy and possessiveness on the part of both individuals; they may become enslaved to impulses that they cannot control.

A disharmonious contact may also trigger in the Venus individual memories of being dominated by the Pluto individual, but then, too, despite the Venus individual having felt threatened, he or she finds it difficult to break free. A vicious cycle of destruction could take shape, particularly if the Venus individual's chart is weak.

MARS-MARS

This aspect has a touch of conflict, competition, and belligerence. When it is manifested harmoniously, the two can harness their egos for the accomplishment of tasks, combine energies and initiatives, and struggle to reach a shared goal.

Because this aspect involves two male planets, even in a male-female relationship there is a sense that the partners are functioning as competing brothers. The clash of egos can create a problem in the shared life of these two, particularly their sex life, because both want to be the initiator. The competition may be either constructive or frustrating and sabotaging, depending upon the planetary constellation as a whole.

When the conjunction forms positive karmic aspects, it shows that these two are continuing shared activity in which they were involved in the past, including possible comradeship in arms. Yet if there is involvement of negative aspects, it may indicate that there was enmity between them that the encounter in this life is meant to settle.

MARS-JUPITER

This aspect indicates friendship between two people. When the contact is harmonious, they feel comfortable in each other's company, and the relationship is neither boring nor pressured. In and of itself, there is no emotional involvement here to complicate things.

Jupiter moderates the activity of Mars, keeping the relationship from becoming too intense. This helps the Mars individual to channel his or her energies more wisely, preventing impulsiveness. This aspect encourages learning in all areas, as well as mutual spiritual growth.

The Mars individual can push the Jupiter individual to take off into the spiritual heights that he or she can reach, serving as a sort of catalyst. In return, the Jupiter individual may teach the Mars individual to see the entire goal, and not only what is right in front of him or her.

A disharmonious conjunction is a catalyst here, transforming the relationship from relaxed to dynamic. The Mars individual spurs the Jupiter individual to form ideas and to realize them, applying them practically. The Jupiter individual, meanwhile, soaks up the Mars individual's aggression and acts under its influence.

When this conjunction forms aspects with karmic planets, it indicates that the Jupiter individual was a consultant to the Mars individual in many areas. It is also likely that they were partners in some political or humanitarian activity or realm.

MARS-SATURN

The Mars individual feels that his or her actions and initiatives are limited by the Saturn individual, who adds a touch of realism and seriousness to the relationship. The Mars individual may be angered because he or she senses that the Saturn individual places obstacles in his or her path; yet deep down, the Mars individual respects the judiciousness and maturity of the Saturn individual, who serves as a model of restraint. The Mars individual knows that control of impulses could be beneficial. The Mars individual, on the other hand, may encourage the Saturn individual to overcome fears and inhibitions that hinder him or her.

When this conjunction is disharmonious, the Mars individual may feel castrated by the Saturn individual's blocking energies, and display impatience of an extreme sort that in turn exacerbates the Saturn individual's stubbornness and rigidity.

In this relationship we see a clear indication of a parent-child or boss-subordinate relationship from the past, as well as patterns in which the Saturn individual restricts yet leads the Mars individual to a path of discipline, perseverance, and goal-setting.

MARS-URANUS

This contact adds thrills and energy to a relationship, and points to both a friendly connection and a strong attraction. In the event that sex is an option here, this aspect signals that there was a magnetic attraction between these two in a past incarnation, which they will rush to consummate in this life.

It may be that these two share an interest in the New Age realm, and possibly encourage each other to act for change. While this is an intense and very dynamic aspect, it does not point to a long-term connection.

This conjunction emphasizes the drive for independence that runs through the blood of both individuals, so that when it is disharmonious, each of them may cling to his or her own path, closing off true cooperation. Furthermore, these two may irritate each other, leading the relationship to be punctuated by angry outbursts. Finally, they may influence each other toward impulsive or irresponsible behavior.

MARS-NEPTUNE

This is an aspect between two planets with totally opposing energies. These two may charm each other at the beginning, but run into difficulties further along. The Neptune individual's dreaminess, gentleness, and sensitivity may contrast with the insensitivity, action orientation, and sparring personality of the Mars individual, creating misunderstandings and frustration. In turn, the Mars individual may lose patience, causing the Neptune individual to feel hurt and misunderstood.

When this relationship works, each can learn a karmic lesson from the other: the Mars individual can encourage the Neptune individual to fulfill his or her ideals and dreams, and can learn from him or her to moderate his or her blunt behavior.

MARS-PLUTO

This is an intensive aspect that, in the case of a couple relationship, inflames the desire of both partners. It also indicates the karmic continuation of a fiery sexual relationship sometime in past lives.

This conjunction expresses dynamism and power. These two encourage each other's initiative and resoluteness. They may also aid each other in implementing ideas and changing courses of action. When it is manifested harmoniously, this conjunction provides positive tension; cooperation can advance these two individual's objectives, whether practical or spiritual.

A disharmonious manifestation of this conjunction can indicate the struggle for dominance in the relationship, and the two may find themselves locked in power struggles. Such an aspect may signal enmity from the past, particularly against a background of the need on both parts for control; any attempt on the part of either one to set limits on the other triggers resistance and resentment. The karmic lesson in this case is to learn to respect each other's free will.

JUPITER-JUPITER

This aspect shows that these two share a worldview and the same outlook on life. This conjunction enables them to expand both their philosophies and look at life in a more carefree way. This is an aspect that adds optimism and tranquility to the relationship, and if it is harmonious, it indicates that in this incarnation they can enjoy the fruits of shared good karma. They may enjoy traveling or studying together, and relations are particularly productive when they both engage in spiritual activity.

JUPITER-SATURN

When this conjunction is manifested harmoniously, this is a balancing aspect in which the Jupiter individual's abundant optimism and drive are under the influence of the Saturnian moderating energy. These two continue an effective, productive cooperation from the past, in which both served as guideposts for each other, though with differing orientations.

When this conjunction is manifested disharmoniously, the Jupiter individual may feel smothered by the Saturnian rigidity. It is likely that they will experience power struggles, because each wants to lead, and their differing styles create divisiveness, which almost certainly began in their past lives in the wake of disagreements based on differences in social, religious, or political beliefs.

JUPITER-URANUS

This aspect indicates considerable potential for shared spiritual growth. Good mental communication and telepathic understanding flow between these two, and the encounter between them aids in the raising of their awareness, sharpens their insight, and sheds new light on issues. Freedom and the search for truth are embodied in this aspect, and both of these individuals sense that their connection enables them freedom of thought with no strings attached.

This aspect indicates the continuation of a friendly connection from past lives in which mental and spiritual growth were central. If this direction is reinforced by other aspects, then these two can accomplish impressive things in the intellectual and spiritual realms, as well as implement social reforms.

A disharmonious conjunction indicates that friction may form between them, and that the initial enthusiasm that they aroused in one another may run its course.

JUPITER-NEPTUNE

This aspect stimulates idealism, the creative urge, and the intuitive capacity. Sympathy and mutual support and encouragement characterize this connection. These two share their feelings and enjoy telepathic communication. This aspect is good for shared spiritual activity, and shows cooperation in past incarnations in either religious or philanthropic organizations and spiritual orders.

When this conjunction is disharmonious, the vision of reality is not focused. The two may disappoint each other as a result of a tendency on both their parts to glamorize reality, and the response may be fatigue and withdrawal into idleness.

JUPITER-PLUTO

This is an intense contact in which the optimism and expanded horizons of Jupiter are combined with the depth and insight of Pluto. This conjunction at its best aids in shared spiritual activity, reawakening in both knowledge of the occult from a past incarnation.

The Jupiter individual aids in expanding and developing the awareness of the Pluto individual, who in turn aids in deepening the spiritual understanding of the Jupiter individual. The connection between these two sharpens in both the capacity for inner vision, as they encourage each other to stay on task.

When these two succeed in uniting their forces constructively, and do not let this aspect's intense energy go to waste, together they can accomplish higher humanitarian objectives and spiritual goals, as well as inspire others to realize their uniqueness.

SATURN-SATURN

When this aspect occurs between two people of the same age, it shows that they have come together to share a karma based on a shared culture and background, and to help each other to understand the karmic meaning of their present-life experiences.

This aspect can also occur between two people whose age difference is about twenty-eight years, and in such a case, the younger one is reliving the karmic experiences of the elder, who can help the younger and add to his or her understanding.

On many occasions, these two are obligated karmically to some tradition or enterprise that they must continue. Because they share a similar approach to tasks and goals, and their ambitions are usually of a similar nature, they also can support each other in paying karmic debts.

When this conjunction is manifested negatively, it can be destructive, as old fears accumulated across incarnations are triggered, creating a double block that is quite difficult to break through. Competition from the past may also be triggered, which can in turn threaten the foundation that these two have built.

Yet when this conjunction is manifested positively, the division of authority between these two is fair; they encourage each other's ambition and aspirations, and march steadily, resolutely, efficiently, and constructively toward the achievement of their goals.

SATURN-URANUS

This aspect symbolizes the culmination of one karmic pattern and the beginning of another. The Saturn individual must develop a new vision of life, and learn to break free of fears of insecurity that are the byproducts of past karma.

When this conjunction is manifested harmoniously, the Saturn individual is willing to change and break loose from the past, while the Uranus individual agrees to enable the Saturn individual to help him or her to streamline and to channel energies, and teach him or her to realize ideas in a practical way.

When this conjunction is disharmonious, it is quite difficult to bridge the gap between these individuals' approaches. Because this aspect is very karmic, and the lesson must be learned, each partner will remain in the relationship for as long as it takes, and will fulfill his or her karmic role. The Saturn individual will mark the goal for the Uranus individual to shoot for, and the Uranus individual will light a fire under the Saturn individual, leading him or her to a crossroads from which he or she will begin to vacillate and change direction.

SATURN-NEPTUNE

This is a contact between two planets with completely different energies, but whose cooperation can be quite productive. The Neptune individual brings with him or her creative energies, and the Saturn individual represents the practical connection between imagination and reality.

The Saturn individual bears for the Neptune individual the karmic lesson that what was envisioned can be realized if one invests effort, imposes self-discipline, and defines the direction and the goal in advance.

This conjunction, when manifested harmoniously, indicates a productive combination of the various tendencies; yet when it is manifested disharmoniously, the Saturn individual's influence can thwart the Neptune individual's creativity and energy.

SATURN-PLUTO

This is a contact between two strong planets, under whose influence each individual forces the other to learn his or her karmic lesson. The Pluto individual forces the Saturn individual to come out of his or her shell and undergo a change. The Pluto individual learns through the relationship to be more practical and productive, and to not waste energy, but instead divert it toward an organized implementation of goals.

When this conjunction is disharmonious, suspicion, competition, and power struggles whose roots lie in past incarnations may mark the relationship; it is therefore their task to cancel such debts in this life.

Conjunctions between the rest of the karmic planets themselves have little personal significance. They appear in charts of those in the same generation, yet have no specific meaning with regard to couplehood.

chapter eight

THE KARMIC HOUSES

At each moment, the wheel is divided into four parts. At the end of each diagonal is a point:
a rising degree and a falling degree; a degree in the upper half and a degree in the lower half.
Call the four points stakes. Divide each into three parts, and these are the twelve houses,
which are most important in a person's nativity.

—Avraham Ibn-Ezra, *Sefer HaTe'amim* (The Book of Reasons), 12th century

From a karmic standpoint, the houses represent life realms that the soul experiences during each of its incarnations. The combination of the meanings of the houses, of the signs on the house cusps, and of the planets that populate the houses enables an understanding of the chart. They describe the person inside and out and what the individual is now as a result of the entirety of his or her lives.

A look at a chart shows houses in which there is an emphasis on work that must be done in this incarnation; some houses indicate abilities, talents, and reserves of skills from the past, while others tell about karmic relationships.

Even if there are empty houses (i.e., houses with no planets in them), this does not mean that the realms represented by these houses are not manifested in this incarnation. In such a case, we must look for the planet ruling the sign that is placed on the cusp of the house, then examine its location and its connections with other planets, and draw the appropriate conclusions.

Astrological calculations enable us to discover in which sign a chart opens. This sign on the eastern horizon is called the ascending sign, or the Ascendant, and its exact degree is determined by the date, place, and exact time of birth. This degree indicates the beginning of the first house and determines the degrees of the cusps of the other houses. This calculation also enables us to locate the planets in the houses.

In the basic division of the wheel of the birth chart, we have two axes—one horizontal and one vertical—that divide the wheel into four parts and form the four "corners," or as Avraham Ibn-Ezra called them, "stakes." The horizontal axis is the *Ascendant-Descendant* axis (ASC/DESC), and the vertical axis is the *Medium Coeli/Imum Coeli* axis (MC/IC). Each of the quarters formed is further divided into three parts, totaling the twelve houses (see figure 9).

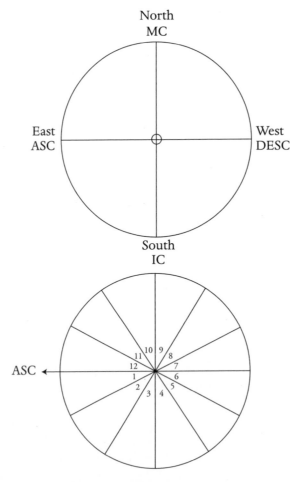

Figure 9—The Horizon/Meridian Axes and the Twelve Houses

The houses, like the signs, incorporate the principle of polarity, and each pair of houses that lie opposite each other on an axis has a common guideline. Esoterically speaking, the axes symbolize energy channels whose role is to attract cosmic abundance toward the life areas represented by the houses. The role of the person represented by the chart is to eliminate blockages, open the channels, and enable abundance to flow and to be absorbed.

In the corners of the chart are four houses of major significance: the first, fourth, seventh, and tenth houses, or the *angular houses*. The first and seventh houses lie at opposite ends of the horizontal axis; this is the *Axis of Identity*, which lies between the house of the "I" and the house of the "other."

The fourth and tenth houses lie at opposite ends of the vertical axis, which constitutes yet another pillar in a person's life. This is the *Axis of Fulfillment*, which lies between the base of the chart, or the House of Roots, and its apex, or the House of Destiny. The other axes are:

- The second/eighth-house axis, or the *Axis of Resources*, lies between the House of Personal Resources and the House of Others' Resources.

- The third/ninth-house axis, or the *Axis of Knowledge*, lies between the House of Information and the House of Knowledge.

- The fifth/eleventh-house axis, or the *Axis of Love*, lies between the House of Self-Love and the House of Universal Love.

- The sixth/twelfth-house axis, or the *Axis of Giving*, lies between the House of Service and the House of Sacrifice.

Further:

- Axes that open in the **fixed signs** (Taurus, Leo, Scorpio, and Aquarius) indicate that the issues that must be treated in the areas symbolized by them are a result of karma that developed over many lives.

- Axes that open in the **cardinal signs** (Aries, Cancer, Libra, and Capricorn) indicate that the issues that must be treated in the areas symbolized by them are a result of close, dominant incarnation.

- When the axes open in the **mutable signs** (Gemini, Virgo, Sagittarius, and Pisces) in the relevant areas, karma is in the process of forming.

THE ANGULAR HOUSES

The cross formed by the two major axes of the angular houses can be likened to a tree. The vertical axis, whose apex is the Midheaven, is analogous to the uppermost branches reaching toward the universe and infinity, while the base of this axis, or the Nadir, is analogous to the roots reaching deep into the earth. The horizontal axis, or Ascendant/Descendant axis, is analogous to the branches reaching to the sides, which enable a person to consolidate his or her identity and achieve inner balance through his or her accessing others.

These two axes represent pillars in a person's life, and the cross that they form is involved in every significant relationship. In comparing two charts, when planets in one chart are in conjunction with the cusps of angular houses in the second chart, it indicates a close relationship between the two individuals; if these planets are karmic, then the relationship has its beginning in past incarnations.

If planets in one chart fall in one of the angular houses in the other chart, it suggests the possibility of a significant relationship between the two individuals, the nature of which can be revealed through the location of the planets and the aspects that they form.

First House: The House of Personality

This house represents the external appearance and physical body of the person, which is the "vehicle" that carries him or her through the present path on Earth. It indicates also the person's state of health, as well as the early conditions of the person's present life.

This house also shows the image that the person chooses to project outward, the first impression that others receive, and the mask or persona that provides protection and aids in forming the person's initial connection with the world.

A person's image is not necessarily the same as his or her inner essence. Often, a person's self-image is affected by others' opinions, particularly when there is not true merging of all parts of the personality. This person's karmic lesson, therefore, is to break free of the outer image and learn to express spontaneously the unique qualities of his or her ascending sign.

The meeting point between a person's inner world represented by his or her chart and the outer world is the ascending degree that opens the first house. This is the most personal and the most sensitive point in the entire horoscope. From an esoteric point of view, the Ascendant is the point at which the soul enters the physical body of the person at the moment of the first breath, and it is also the point at which the soul becomes linked to the subtler bodies of the person.

The person represented by the chart chose to undergo in this incarnation various experiences, certain of which are the continuation or reenactment of experiences from other incarnations, and others of which are new. The ascending sign, the planet that rules the Ascendant, and the planets in the first house all express the experiences in this incarnation that enable the person to differentiate him- or herself, and to undergo new experiences that the soul has not yet undergone. They also show how the incarnating soul faces the world, how it will cope with the life circumstances in which it finds itself, and how it will adapt itself—against the backdrop of the entirety of its past lives—to its present life. This house is directly related to the here and now.

The first house shows the means available to the person for building and establishing an identity; one of these means is encounters with others. Because the first house represents the impression a person makes, it also represents his or her effect on others. Because this house is also related to the physical body, it shows the degree of physical attraction between the person represented by the chart and the person whose planets are in contact with this house. A chart comparison will show what the response to an encounter will be—if the response is steady or passing, and, if there is chemistry between them, whether the relationship will continue.

A connection between planets in one chart and the first house in a second shows that the planet individual affects the shaping of the personality and self-image of the first-house individual. A harmonious connection awakens excitement and empathy between the two, while a disharmonious connection arouses irritation or even revulsion.

When karmic planets in one chart are connected with the first house of another chart, it shows an inevitable influence that has continued since past incarnations. It is hard to break free of this influence, which is still active, and whose role is to trigger memories that are beneficial for new experiences and learning in this life.

Harmonious connections show an undying attraction that brings excitement to both sides. Disharmonious connections indicate tension whose roots lie in the past and that will be expressed in this life based on the nature of the activating planet.

The Seventh House: The House of the Other

This house represents karma that is connected to our relationships with partners and others. A person's purpose is to merge harmoniously all parts of the personality; through encounters with others, he or she receives the opportunity to get to know his or her positive sides, make them conscious, and assimilate them into a whole.

This house represents how we relate to others and experience them in our lives, what we expect of others even if we are not conscious of our expectations, and how others can fill our needs. This house also represents the karmic circumstances that shape the way we relate to partnership. It also represents the partner, through whom we learn our karmic lessons, and our partner who can help us to achieve repair or karmic balance.

The seventh house lies opposite the first house, and serves as a mirror that reflects facets of ourselves that are unknown to us, yet which can be revealed through a partner. A completing partner can enable us to see clearly our hidden facets and to fully acknowledge them.

However, if disharmonious aspects are involved in the connection, sympathy can turn into antipathy. Oppositions, for example, can be manifested in approach-avoidance relations, and can even point to the possibility of divorce.

The position of the seventh house (i.e., the positions of the planets connected to it, and the aspects that they form) show how the person deals with couplehood and partnership. When planets from one chart fall in the seventh house of a second chart, or form aspects with the ruler of the seventh house of the second chart, there is an immediate attraction between these two.

Karmic planets from one chart that are connected to the seventh house of another chart indicate an incarnational relationship. When Saturn is involved, we have before us a clearly karmic relationship whose nature will be revealed according to the aspects formed, and their degree of benefit depends upon the level of spiritual evolution of the individuals involved. Also, aspects formed between Venus and karmic planets connected with this house show marriage between these individuals in the past.

The Fourth House: The House of Roots

This house is the base of the horoscope, and shows the foundation upon which our lives stand, where we began our growth, and what the purpose is of our evolution in this life.

The fourth house represents our instinctual sense of belonging and our roots, including parents, family, home, country, tradition, and heritage, through which our inner sense of security and our emotional foundations are formed. This house also shows our past, both in this life and in past incarnations, and the imprint it has left on our present lives.

Here in the fourth house we can learn of the family karma that awaits our soul when it enters this world, and of our parents, to whom we chose to be born as per experiences in the family realm that we decided to undergo. Naturally, our relationships with others are affected by this decision, and as such this house also shows how this choice will affect the family that we ourselves form.

When planets from one chart fall in the fourth house of another, it shows how these two individuals will respond to each other in a home environment. The aspects formed with planets connected to the fourth house will naturally add to this information. The Moon, the natural ruler of the fourth house, will also give us valuable information about the family factors that have left their imprint on this person.

Karmic planets in one chart connected to the fourth or tenth house in another can indicate cross-incarnational familial relationships—particularly parent-child—between the two individuals. The aspects formed by planets in these houses show whether these were good relationships or difficult ones that require more work.

The Tenth House: The House of Destiny

The tenth house represents the social status of the person represented by the chart, the degree of respect that he or she receives from others, and the career through which the individual fulfills ambitions and makes his or her contribution to society. It symbolizes not only the person's goals and professional image, but also the peak of his or her ambition, the search for an ideal self-image, and the destiny that is his or her karma to fulfill in this life.

The tenth house also symbolizes those who represent authority to this person. In addition, it symbolizes the mother or the dominant parent in the family constellation. Planets connected to this house indicate the nature of the relationship with these same authority figures. In addition, outer planets add a karmic dimension to the relationship and indicate its nature, both in this life and past lives.

In chart comparison, the aspects formed between planets in both charts show whether the second individual—either the parent or the partner that we chose—helps us to realize our potential and consolidate our position and self-image; whether he or she pushes us to achieve in a constructive way, or thwarts us by dominating us. It is also likely that we either admire or fear this person, causing us to regress in our ability to realize our potential on our own.

Contact between outer planets in the second chart and our tenth house shows a pattern from our karmic past of the other person dominating us. In the case of a romantic relationship, such a contact may represent a reminder of a past pattern of a parent-child relationship that existed between the two partners. When a chart comparison shows a close connection between both tenth houses, it indicates that both individuals share a karmic destiny for whose sake they have met in this life.

THE AXIS OF RESOURCES AND VALUES

Second House

The second house is represented by the element of earth, and is related to the consolidation of the soul in the material world, and to the tangible things that may appeal to it in this world. This house therefore represents a person's material assets and his or her financial situation.

From a karmic standpoint, this house represents the resources and skills with which the person was equipped in past incarnations, and which could aid him or her in the present life. The position of this person's house (i.e., the position of the planets located in it or ruling it) shows whether the incarnating soul chose a life of material abundance or lack, and how the person relates to either.

The second house is traditionally ruled by Venus, which represents values and feelings. In an esoteric sense, it symbolizes not only material values, but spiritual values as well, and also the multitude of feelings from past lives. Therefore, this house has importance when comparing charts of couples.

When planets that rule the second house or are located in it form aspects with Jupiter, Saturn, or Pluto in a second chart, it indicates that in a past incarnation these two shared an involvement in either business, properties, or finances. In addition, when planets from one chart fall in the second house of the second chart, it indicates the degree of contribution of the first-chart individual to the financial and emotional in/security of the second individual. Karmic planets that fall here show a karmic debt between these two—either emotional or financial—that must be balanced. The planets involved show the means for achieving this balance.

Eighth House

This house is related to the birth-death cycle, rebirth, spiritual powers, and the capacity for true transformation of one's life. The motifs of death and transformation are themselves related, because the death of one's old ego is a necessary process for any significant personality change, and every physical death opens up an opportunity for a soul to transform.

The eighth house also represents the material, mental, and spiritual resources of others, and therefore shows in what way the person will share his or her life with others, what the person contributes, and what he or she receives through contact with others. Because this house also represents sexuality and desires, it shows the nature of the person's emotional and sexual relationships with others.

The other individual's planets, which activate this house, have a strong effect on many levels of activity. They stimulate the physical realm, i.e., sexual and monetary urges, as well as the psychological and the spiritual. The way in which this activity is manifested depends on the nature of the planets activating the house, and on the aspects that they form.

In a chart comparison, when aspects are formed between the planets that are connected with the eighth house in one chart and outer planets in the other chart, it can indicate that the two individuals were involved in past lives in either monetary or business dealings. Harmonious aspects show that they can comfortably continue this productive cooperation, or can support each other monetarily.

Disharmonious aspects point to karmic conflicts whose background is monetary, such as an inheritance, or a disagreement concerning alimony. Conflicts from the karmic past stemming from sexual problems are also likely. Disharmonious aspects can also indicate sexual obsessions triggered by activation of this house by planets from the second chart, particularly if Pluto is involved.

All conflicts herein must be resolved in this life. Otherwise, the problems will run even deeper, dragging bad karma with the individuals into the next life.

If the individuals involved are romantic partners, and both are working on developing their spirituality and awareness, then they will have the desire to resolve problems of the past constructively and effectively. A shared interest in the occult and in developing mystical powers can enliven the relationship and inspire high levels of cooperation and intimacy. A special experience awaits these two in the sexual sphere, with their sexual relationship possibly even lifting them to new spiritual heights.

THE AXIS OF MENTALITY AND KNOWLEDGE

Third House

The primary sphere dealt with in this house is our relationship with our environment and everyday surroundings. Other spheres are mental powers, verbal skills, basic knowledge, transportation, and communication.

On the karmic level, this house can indicate problems manifested in communications and movement, such as stuttering, muteness, or deafness, or even blindness, lameness, or physical or mental disabilities whose roots actually lie in a trauma from a past incarnation that is still manifesting itself in the present.

In a chart comparison, aspects between planets connected with the third house in both charts shows a strong mental influence. Such a contact between charts may indicate that these two share an intellectual interest in certain areas. The nature of the aspects show whether the mental communication between these two is productive and fluent, or if there are disruptions, or if the relationship is sensed by one or both of them as restrictive or annoying.

Planets in one chart relating to the third house in another chart can reveal a teacher-pupil relationship from the incarnational past, as this house represents the transmission of information. It can also show shared karma as family members, since the third house also represents relatives. The relevant aspects show the nature of such a relationship.

Ninth House

This house represents expansion, development, and spiritual enlightenment, which are naturally ruled by Jupiter, the planet of abundance, broad horizons, vision, and the re-awakening of the spirit. This house reveals the ideal according to which a person must direct him- or herself, so that he or she can achieve spiritual insights.

This house also represents ethical, philosophical, or religious attitudes that the person solidified in past lives and that affect his or her ideas, positions, and worldview in this life; as well as his or her relationships in which religious, philosophical, and educational issues assume importance.

A chart comparison will show whether these two individuals agree on their worldview. Outer planets in one chart that activate the ninth house in the second chart can indicate the karmic effect of a religious or spiritual guide that helped to shape the spiritual world of the ninth-house individual.

The influence of karmic planets (except Saturn) can indicate telepathic communication and an ongoing spiritual relationship from the past that continues to inspire both individuals mentally and spiritually.

THE AXIS OF LOVE AND FRIENDSHIP

Fifth House

The main issues of the fifth house are love and romance, children, and creativity. This house shows how we relate to these, how they are manifested in our lives, and what gives us pleasure and joy.

From a karmic perspective, just as the fourth house shows which parents the person chose to be born to, so does the fifth house show which children will choose us as parents. Because this is also the house that represents romantic relationships, it can also show us loves from past lives who in this incarnation are born as parent and child.

Lastly, this house can show us the creative talents that a person brings from past incarnations, and that are incumbent upon him or her to continue to nurture and realize in this life in order to achieve gratification.

Planets in one chart that influence the other's fifth house can either stimulate or limit creative and romantic expression.

When Mars and Venus influence this house together with outer planets connected to the fourth or tenth house, it may indicate the existence of romantic relationships in past lives between the individual and his or her offspring in this life. The Sun's or the Moon's influence on the fifth house may indicate the parent in the present life having been a lover in a past incarnation.

Eleventh House

This house represents friends, colleagues, and fellow members of groups, and focuses on karma connected to a person's relations with acquaintances as well as his or her community. The position of this house reveals the person's degree of social involvement, his or her contribution to the community, and his or her ability to realize ambitions and advance goals that are not related to personal gain but rather to the good of the community or of humanity.

In comparing charts, the outer planets from one chart falling in the eleventh house of the second chart can indicate that there was a social relationship, friendship, or membership in the same organization in the past, and their encounter in this incarnation is meant to complete social or humanitarian tasks begun in the past.

Harmonious aspects show a possible productive continuation of past-life shared activity, and these two may be involved in some group activity in the present connected with science, a humanitarian cause, or the occult sciences.

If the aspects with outer planets are disharmonious, it may indicate that this relationship in the past was marred. It is likely that in a past incarnation there was intrigue, dishonesty, or exploitation between these two, and they parted in a state of enmity.

The initial thrill of the relationship brought them back to the present relationship, yet past patterns may return along with it, and resentment could erupt anew unless they can rise above the jealousy, intrigues, and vested interests, and behave with awareness for the sake of repairing and balancing their relationship.

THE AXIS OF GIVING AND SERVING

Sixth House

The sixth house deals with health, hygiene, and nutrition; serving others; and a person's relationship to his or her job and as a boss to his or her subordinates. This house is also important in understanding karma connected to work and the workplace. Therefore, in a chart comparison, regarding work, the way that this house is activated shows how the two individuals communicate in the workplace.

Because the sixth house also deals with illness as well as serving, when it is activated by planets from another chart, it can indicate a patient-caregiver relationship rooted in past lives. Understanding the deeper meaning of this house is important emotionally and spiritually, as illnesses are actually warnings that we may overlook at the expense of our innermost parts, or even of our spiritual needs.

The sixth house is related to physical ailments of karmic origin whose beginnings lie in previous existences. Certain illnesses have their roots in traumas from a past life, and only discovery of the trauma can enable the person to cure the illness. By the same token, illnesses and accidents are chosen by the soul as a guaranteed way to balance karma. Some souls choose to undergo physical hardship or disabilities in order to experience what they caused someone in another life.

A soul can also choose to reexperience illness or injury so that it can learn this time around to treat these constructively, or as a means to spiritual awakening. Indeed, many people who have experienced a clinical death following an accident or during an illness have undergone a crucial turnabout in their lives leading to a spiritual awakening. A soul may even choose to undergo such experiences in order to change negative attitudes imprinted on it, giving it the opportunity to develop qualities such as endurance of suffering, unyielding optimism, and acceptance of fate.

The subject of acceptance of fate and overcoming the desires of the ego is closely related to the sixth house, which represents the level of our ability to serve others and devote ourselves to them humbly and without expectation of recompense. Spiritual growth can take place not only through personally experiencing an illness, but also through a close connection with someone who is ill, and caring for him or her.

There are cases of children devoting themselves to the care of their parents, or parents who care for their children with disabilities, wherein the care itself elevates the caregiver to a higher level. In other cases, parents of children with mental retardation, Down's syndrome, or autism are being given an opportunity to experience devotion and unconditional love many times over.

Still others use their personal suffering for the greater good by establishing a support group or organization to help others in the same situation. Or, there are those who, having lost a loved one, use their bereavement as an impetus for spiritual growth and devote themselves to serving others.

The sixth house therefore represents all acts performed not for the sake of reward, and the extent of our ability to persevere in attending to the needs of others altruistically and out of pure motives rather than personal gain.

Twelfth House

The twelfth house is closely related to the concept of karma, because it represents the unconscious, which contains the entirety of memories and mental and emotional patterns of a soul's past. This house represents the hidden that must be revealed in this life; repressed issues that must be dealt with; unresolved problems of past lives; and weaknesses that have gained a foothold in our subconscious over incarnations.

Karmic planets connected to the twelfth house symbolize powers beyond our control, with which we find it difficult to cope on a conscious level. The way to deal with these is to tune in to cosmic energies. The twelfth house also represents seclusion in all its forms, whether forced upon us or of our own volition. It represents solitude, solitary places, and periods of withdrawal during which a person may make contact with his or her inner self.

This house indicates karmic relationships between the person and spiritual teachers who help him or her to tune in to and elucidate his or her inner self, and to stimulate the aspirations to achieve awareness and spiritual powers. Further in this direction, the twelfth house represents meditation and other means of raising our awareness, developing our mystical abilities, our yearning for ultimate peace, and our desire to unite with the cosmic consciousness.

The striving to achieve awareness includes the effort to be conscious of the *shadow*. In Jungian terms, our shadow is the dark side of our personality, which is hidden from our consciousness. Illuminating the shadow is necessary, both for our personal development and for our capacity to create healthy relationships. Contact with others enables us to get in touch with our shadow, due to our tendency to project it onto others, and to attribute to others our negative traits.

In a chart comparison, planets in the second individual's chart that fall in our twelfth house aid us in revealing and shedding light on the repressed and dark parts of our personality. In doing so, we can act to eliminate them.

The seventh house—the house of couplehood—also plays a role in our understanding of the unconscious, yet the twelfth house deals with much deeper content, and therefore the effect of the planets from the second chart that are related to the twelfth house is much stronger.

When the twelfth house is activated in a couple's relationship, their way of relating to the relationship is emotional, and their sensitivity is at its highest. In such a relationship, the partners do not seek the external, as they do in a relationship based on the physical or the material; rather, they are interested in inner values and nonverbal communication.

In a relationship in which the twelfth house is involved, both psychological and karmic patterns are at work. The person's complexes are triggered, and if the activation is by disharmonious aspects, it can indicate neurotic tendencies that if not treated may cause depression, self-destruction, withdrawal from reality, or suicidal tendencies.

When the activation is by harmonious aspects, then repressed neuroses can be treated and their negative effects eliminated. Harmonious aspects indicate an emotional connection between these two; they are in tune with each other, and they enjoy intuitive and telepathic communication. Partners who are spiritually evolved may show an interest in mysticism, meditate together, and enjoy shared spiritual experiences.

CHAPTER NINE

THERE'S A DRAGON
IN THE HOUSE

The starting point conceals within it all time segments.
The unsealed past, the everlasting present, the latent future,
Are facets of the same essence
That has no end and no beginning.

—RUTH AHARONI

Indeed, we have a dragon in the houses of the birth chart: it has a head, a tail . . . and even a beard—it reflects a long history of incarnations. Via the Dragon, we can see our present life as part of a continuing chain. Understanding the meanings of the Dragon's Head and Tail enables us to discover the path that the incarnating soul has chosen to tread. The rest of the chart gives information on how the person makes his or her way on this path.

The Dragon's Head and Tail, also called the Moon's nodes, are astronomical points considered esoteric in their nature. These nodes are formed by the meeting point of the Moon's path with the Sun's path. The North Node, or the *Dragon's Head*, is the point at which the Moon passes from the southern latitude to the northern latitude. The South Node, or the *Dragon's Tail*, is the point at which the Moon passes from the northern latitude to the southern latitude.

Just as the Moon in a birth chart is ultimately important in understanding a person's life, so do the Moon's Nodes have great significance in understanding the life of the soul, and the karmic purpose of incarnating can be revealed through the nodes.

These points lie at two ends of an axis that actually serves as a bridge between the past and the future. The Dragon's Tail shows what was learned in past incarnations, and transmits the influence of karma along the axis, enabling its use via the Dragon's Head, and which should be treated in this life.

The Dragon defines the karmic lessons that a soul has chosen to learn in this life, as well as the repairs that he or she must execute. The locations of the Dragon's Head and Tail link the person with his or her past and show the way to the future. The Dragon's Head and Tail each have a magnetic attraction that acts upon a person, pulling him or her in the chosen direction.

The Dragon's Tail symbolizes the sum total of a person's past, including events, ideas, attitudes, and thoughts from every incarnation, whose cumulative influence and unresolved problems therefrom come together to create the present life as it is lived. The Tail pushes us to act instinctively, according to subconscious patterns imprinted on us, and it returns us to old behaviors. The Tail actually constitutes a template for everything repeated an infinite number of times and is imprinted on the incarnating soul.

Our most negative traits are actually those that we carry with us for thousands of years of incarnations, during which we allow them to set down roots in our souls. Behaviors of the past affect a person in a constant way, and the temptation to fall into past patterns is so strong that a small step backward can set us back so far that considerable strength—and often help—is needed to pull ourselves out of the abyss.

Because it is so hard to change behaviors that have been imprinted on us for so long, we have a tendency to rest on our haunches, because this is a comfortable and familiar position, but in fact, to flow with changes is much easier than it is to resist them.

The Dragon's Head symbolizes the future and the renewal of life, as well as an experience that we have not yet undergone. It also suggests a future direction that a person senses instinctively.

The Dragon's Head represents the highest realm of experience that can be reached, but we cannot reach it as long as we have not broken free of the Tail. In order to do so, we must give up on each of the old, negative behaviors that has taken root in our lives, as well as of those memories that have no benefit for us. This is also the case regarding karmic relationships whose time is passed, but that we hold onto, though they no longer serve us.

The transition from the Tail to the Head is a turning point from a state of subconscious response to a state of conscious choice. Conscious choice liberates the soul from helplessness and dependence on external forces; it brings about change, which in turn creates new possibilities.

If the initial response of the incarnating soul is to behave according to the Dragon's Tail, then the demands of the Head are for change, growth, and new behaviors. An occasional return to the past is not a bad thing, but it should be only a "rest stop," or a familiar time-out for the soul that is making progress. Yet dwelling on the old creates blockages on the path to transcendence; leaving the past behind is necessary for growth. It is incumbent upon us to leave behind our limiting behaviors, fears, and negative thought patterns if we are to move forward. Only the understanding that these tether us can enable us to move forward with momentum.

The locations of the Dragon's Head and Tail in the signs and in the various houses enable us to understand the karma of our present life, and show how these energies are manifested. Every location enables the soul to experience a different karmic facet, and to better understand its karmic purpose. Thus the soul can fulfill itself, implement the required repairs, and achieve inner completeness and harmony.

THE DRAGON IN SIGNS AND HOUSES

There are many similarities between the meaning of the location of the Dragon in a certain house and the meaning of its location in the sign that naturally rules that house. Therefore, a combined interpretation of the Dragon's Head and Tail in a sign and in the house ruled by the sign are given here. The relevant interpretation can be obtained through a combination of the influences of the houses in which the Dragon is located, and those of the signs in which it is located. Let's take, for example, a woman whose Dragon's Tail in her chart is located in the first house and in Capricorn; her Dragon's Head is exactly opposite—in the seventh house and in Cancer (see figure 10).

The meaning of this combination may be thus: In a past incarnation, this woman's energy, and attention were focused on establishing her identity and fulfilling her personal needs (Tail in the first house), her career, earning people's respect, and acquiring status (Tail in Capricorn). She accomplished this, however, at the expense of her family life and relationship with a partner, because the latter require considering the needs of others.

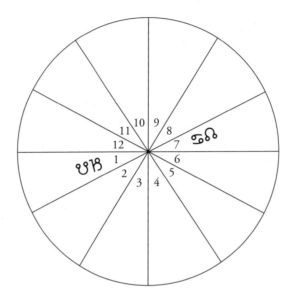

Figure 10—The Dragon's Head and Tail

In this life, this woman must work diligently at building a home (Head in Cancer) and nurturing her relationship with a partner (Head in the seventh house), and channel her energies in a balanced fashion toward a career that does not come at the expense of those close to her.

Tables showing the locations of the Dragon's Head and Tail in the various signs every year from 1900–2000 appear in appendix A.

Head in Aries or First House; Tail in Libra or Seventh House

The basic karmic purpose of the soul is to individuate, yet not fall into the trap of self-centeredness. In previous incarnations, this person did not develop his or her identity enough; the individual based his or her world on that of those close to him or her. In this life, too, while there is a tendency to continue to base his or her identity on that of others', the person has been given a chance to find his or her true self. In order to do so, the individual must discover who he or she truly is; the person must come to understand that the meaning of "I" does not rest on others' identities, and that self-worth is not based only on others' esteem.

This person's self-esteem in the past did not enable him or her to choose a direction autonomously, and now the individual must overcome the vacillation, reluctance, fears, and lack of self-esteem that were his or her lot before, and act to establish a unique direction of his or her own. Because this process can create difficulties in a couple's relationship, this person must take care not to regress to behavior patterns of giving in and compromising for the sake of peace, as he or she did in the past.

The goal in this axis is to find the right balance, so that establishing one's independence and living one's personal values must not take place at the expense of emotional and partnership harmony.

Head in Taurus or Second House; Tail in Scorpio or Eighth House

The karmic goal in this axis is to develop solid values that will withstand both the spiritual and material tests of time. Many of the life situations of an individual with this axis are ruled by the subconscious. In previous incarnations, this person behaved obsessively and intensely and wasted energy on life's dark side, and his or her path was littered with crises and setbacks.

Memories of difficult times are imprinted on this person's subconscious, causing the individual inner disquiet that he or she does not understand, as well as a feeling of "no way out." This person must learn to act with moderation and take it slowly, forging an inner peace that enables clear vision. He or she must learn not to look back, a tendency that can taint efforts earnestly made and intensify self-destructive impulses.

One important lesson that this person must learn is not to use material goods or sex as a means to control others. This person must liberate him- or herself from possessiveness and jealousy, which are the consequences of insecurity. The individual must internalize the truth that the abundance of the universe will suffice, and there is no need to hoard; if he or she opens the energy channels that are blocked by lower impulses, then abundance will flow effortlessly. This person must come to the realization that true riches are one's inner values, and these must be shared lovingly with others.

Head in Gemini or Third House; Tail in Sagittarius or Ninth House

The karmic goal of this axis is to develop communication and public-speaking skills. The person with this axis must learn to communicate with those around him or her, and to bring the superior ideas that occupy him or her down to an everyday level so that others can absorb them. In addition, this person must develop the ability to distinguish between goals that are beyond his or her reach and realistic goals.

Freedom is crucial to this person, and therefore he or she tries to avoid constraints. Yet if the individual's life circumstances entail obligations that he or she cannot escape, then an inner disquiet may increase to such an extent that he or she becomes apathetic and shirks all responsibility. In an effort to calm the inner storms, the person may occupy him- or herself with too many duties and end up focusing on none.

The sense of duality is strong in this axis; the past has taught this person to see both sides of every issue. In previous incarnations, this person learned to view the world with a broad philosophy; he or she worked at evolving spiritually and accumulating knowledge. In this incarnation, the person must implement that knowledge in the everyday routine, the goal being to transmit it and pass on his or her wisdom to others.

Head in Cancer or Fourth House; Tail in Capricorn or Tenth House

This axis shows that this soul entered this world with inner pride, and in a past incarnation, was invested in earning respect, acknowledgement, and admiration; honor and prestige continue to motivate this person subconsciously and influence all activity in this incarnation. This person continues to aspire to prove his or her self-worth, yet fear of failure is also imprinted on him or her. Therefore, whenever the individual feels that he or she is not living up to his or her own standards, he or she chooses to avoid meeting the challenge, thereby avoiding experiences and blocking off the opportunity to overcome limitations and obstacles.

This person has become used to suppressing feelings and hiding weaknesses, and does not let others get close. In this life, the individual must break down the walls that he or she has built, tune in to his or her emotions, and allow him- or herself to give to and receive from others. The person must also learn to accept his or her weaknesses, as well as those of others, and not to exploit those who do show weakness.

A person with this axis is conflicted to one degree or another about finding a balance between the demands of family and the demands of career. At some stage in his or her life, the individual will try to break free of the yoke of family, but the mental yoke will come off only when the person understands that he or she needs the emotional warmth that a family can provide, and that the family connection is a necessary condition for success in the world.

The karmic purpose of this axis is to develop the capacity for nurturing and giving, not only materially and out of a sense of obligation but also out of sensitivity, tenderness, and a sense of reciprocity. In addition, this person must learn to balance between justice and mercy, and perfect the art of compassion and forgiveness.

Head in Leo or Fifth House; Tail in Aquarius or Eleventh House

The karmic goal of this axis is to resolve conflicts between the head and the heart, and to merge the inclinations of both constructively. The soul must learn to balance between emotional withdrawal and involvement. In past incarnations, this person developed the "art of detachment" and felt free to act independently; yet this detachment did not enable the effective implementation of his or her ideas. Despite the fact that the individual was motivated by them, he or she lacked the strength to transform ideas into reality, and most of them remained within the realm of vision.

In this incarnation, this person must develop willpower and self-discipline, and combine creativity with performance. Only then will the individual come to know that he or she is capable of realizing ambitions, and that he or she has the ability to create a world based on his or her dreams.

This person takes pride in his or her uniqueness, and despite the fact that the need for solitude is imprinted upon him or her, this individual also must gather people around him or her, to rebuild him- or herself through their responses and appreciation. This person must learn the art of love in all its manifestations, not only in a general sense but also by opening him- or herself up to both physical love and intimate relationships. Thus the individual will be able to realize the karmic goal of balance between love for humanity and personal love.

Head in Virgo or Sixth House; Tail in Pisces or Twelfth House

The lesson to be learned by the person with this axis is to take responsibility and to develop a discriminating sense. Despite his or her high ideals and spiritual abilities in the incarnational past, this person did not have his or her feet on the ground, and therefore found it difficult to complete his or her tasks. In addition, the inclination to become emotionally involved in everything he or she did sabotaged this person's ability to perform.

Now this person must demonstrate diligence, organizational skills, and the ability to stick to a goal. He or she must begin to attend to implementing ideas in the earthly realm, and to confront the necessity to be disciplined, efficient, and effective. In addition, the individual must learn to take responsibility not only for his or her deeds and physical welfare but also for his or her soul and thoughts, while understanding that mental imbalance means imbalance in the body and the outer world as well.

A large part of the work of repairing this person's karma must be done in a closed facility, where, by mobilizing on the behalf of others, the individual can also help him- or herself. It is likely that in past incarnations this person experienced physical and emotional imprisonment, the imprint of which is still in him or her, along with phobias and paranoia. Therefore, the person must keep working at building trust in him- or herself and in others.

The karmic task of this axis is to serve out of love. This individual must not only act out of obligation, but also tune in to the universal will whose goal is moving the world through time by unconditional and limitless love.

Head in Libra or Seventh House; Tail in Aries or First House

In this axis, intensive learning must take place about the needs of others and self-sacrifice. The karmic goal here is to learn true cooperation with others, and channeling energetic resources to serve them. Selflessness should guide this person, who must take care not to overnurture his or her own ego.

This axis is paradoxical, as this person feels a strong urge to gratify his or her own needs first, and only when the individual has sated them can he or she turn to gratifying others. Because self-gratification can last a lifetime, this person must learn to divert his or her attention to others, to notice their needs, to develop sensitivity to them, to listen to them and consider their opinions, and to be open to ways that differ from his or her own. The individual must moderate his or her opinionatedness to which he or she became accustomed during a previous incarnation, and learn to see the other side of the coin in every issue.

In a past incarnation, this person was invested in developing independence and nurturing uniqueness, and he or she finds it difficult to give up on these. If the water element is emphasized in the individual's chart, it may make this easier, but if the fire element is dominant, then the person faces a hard lesson of mastering a stubborn ego. Patience and tolerance for others and their opinions is the first step in spiritual progress. This person must open his or her heart to constant giving, because in this life he or she has been given the opportunity to work on repairing karmic relationships from the past through balancing relations with people whom karma has placed around him or her.

Head in Scorpio or Eighth House; Tail in Taurus or Second House

In this axis, the soul must learn to share its insights and material and mental resources with others. This is not an easy task, as in previous lives, this person labored under a heavy burden of earthly obligations, and was occupied with material issues, and as if that weren't enough, the individual is also plagued by an inner sense of dissatisfaction that embitters his or her life.

This axis indicates stubbornness and fixation; this person finds it difficult, even painful, to change behavior patterns. The individual's growth will start only when he or she learns to break free of old patterns and from the craving to accumulate goods. Growth is based on the ability to accept change in oneself and one's life, and not to get stuck in patterns that may have served one in the past but have no more use in the present.

This axis emphasizes the unending circle of life, of birth, death, and rebirth, through which the soul learns that it can undergo many beginnings and endings in one lifetime, and to take from its depths the strength to be reborn and to renew itself. The karmic purpose of the individual with this axis is to learn to strengthen his or her spiritual self by overcoming lust, possessiveness, and materialism, and by placing his or her confidence in the power of the universe to provide for his or her needs. The individual must also adhere to mystical wisdom, because it is from here that he or she can draw the strength needed for transformation and rebirth.

The spiritual work that this person faces is to eliminate the superfluous in his or her life, until what is left is pure existence; only then will the individual feel that this is his or her most valuable possession.

Head in Sagittarius or Ninth House; Tail in Gemini or Third House

A soul with this axis is attracted to philosophy, religion, and mysticism, as well as both physical and spiritual journeys. The karmic goal herein is the search for meaning. A person with this axis is restless and feels a constant need to search; constant activity and change are a must for him or her. Duality here is strong, even reaching instability.

In past lives, this person was not anchored to a physical place, and did not solidify his or her ideas. The individual feared commitment and permanence, and felt a strong need to keep all options open out of a fear of missing out. In a previous incarnation, the person craved people's company; therefore, despite needing freedom now, he or she is still attracted almost involuntarily to people, and as a result sometimes finds him- or herself in relationships that are not a good fit.

This person aspires to stretch his or her understanding to its limits; therefore, he or she seeks experiences that are ever more stimulating spiritually. This individual came to this life to realize a philosophical vision, to learn to see both the details in the picture and the picture as a whole, and to move from sophistication to wisdom. The person's main karmic lesson is to acquire knowledge by tuning in to his or her higher self.

Head in Capricorn or Tenth House; Tail in Cancer or Fourth House

This axis deals with the conflict between the inner world of the soul imprinted with hurtful memories and overdependence on family, and the outer world in which the soul seeks gratification, specifically through establishing a social position and career achievement. The person with this axis must develop a tougher skin and a more reasoned thought process in order to skim off the mass of feelings due to which he or she loses proportion. The individual must overcome oversensitivity and sentimentality, as well as a fear of loss.

In former lives, this person was occupied with family, and home was the center of gravity. The individual came to this life with a large familial debt, and therefore finds him- or herself devoting a lot of time to family. This sense of obligation, though, causes him or her to feel chained, and also triggers past feelings of helplessness. This person feels that he or she does not always have the strength to bear the burden, and that he or she wants to go back to being protected and cared for by others.

This axis offers this person a painful yet worthwhile process for growth. The individual can break free of the sense of helplessness, bondage, and fear of enjoyment if only he or she comes to understand that his or her karmic role is to provide shelter for others. The person must understand that every person whom he or she must care for enables him or her to pay back a debt that will remove an obstacle to growth.

This person must internalize the understanding of true responsibility, and learn to trust and depend on him- or herself and achieve self-knowledge and self-control. The individual can then realize selfhood and autonomy, and gain authority in the outer world.

Head in Aquarius or Eleventh House; Tail in Leo or Fifth House

In this axis, the soul learns to develop devotion to all of humanity. In former lives, this individual saw him- or herself as the center of the universe and "spun" on the "me axis." In this incarnation, the person came to this world with arrogance, as well as a formidable inner strength that he or she used to dominate others, for whom he or she had little regard and a patronizing attitude. Now this person must learn to consider others and form connections with them as equals.

In this life, this person must learn to overcome egocentrism. In the past, the individual wasted love energy on him- or herself, on the worth of his or her ego, and on casual affairs, particularly if the Dragon's Tail is located in the fifth house. The person became his or her own worst enemy, because egocentrism creates energy blockages on the path to self-fulfillment.

This person must therefore learn the value of true friendship. In the past, the individual valued external splendor, and gathered glamorous people around him or her to serve as ornaments, yet their friendship was not real. Now the person must divert attention away from him- or herself toward others. The individual must learn the value of the common welfare, and his or her ambitions should be realized for the common benefit and not only for his or her own gratification. Otherwise, despite power and prestige, this person will be perpetually frustrated.

In this life, this person must find a balance between reaching personal goals and serving humanitarian causes. The individual must learn to see humanity as one big family, and harness his or her will for the sake of greater goals.

Head in Pisces or Twelfth House; Tail in Virgo or Sixth House

This axis places the soul in a difficult situation wherein the person is torn between two directions that appear contradictory: the spiritual and the material. In past lives, this person lived in a defined, structured world made up of details. The individual was a perfectionist and functioned in a practical, methodical manner. He or she was also critical of those around him or her. Now the aspiration to reach perfection rules the person, and he or she finds it difficult to cope. This world is far from the cozy habitat of past incarnations, and does not give the individual the satisfaction that he or she craves.

Because this person now understands that the world deviates from the limits of logic and sense—that there is another world beyond—he or she begins to understand things not cognitively but rather through gut instinct and intuition. The individual wants to experience the esoteric, which is the opposite of what he or she knew or permitted him- or herself to know in the past. However, at the same time, the person finds it difficult to shake off his or her old beliefs that divided the world into pigeonholes, creating the danger that the individual will fall back into his or her old analytical ways, which disrupt free flow and spontaneity.

This axis epitomizes the dichotomy of one part of the soul holding on to limitations of the past and the other part striving for infinity. This person is weary of the demands of the physical world, and has come to realize that it is not the orderly place that he or she once thought it was. This disintegration of the sense of order may lead this person to chaos, which may in turn cause an existential crisis, seclusion, or a withdrawal.

This danger of "dropping out" may lead this person to the edge; he or she has a tendency to enter the karmic reservoir and draw from it difficult experiences involving suffering. Part of the karma that this soul chooses will be connected to closed facilities, some of which he or she is in involuntarily, some voluntarily, some as a patient, and some as a caregiver. If this person is a caregiver, his or her contact with others will differ from that of the past. In the past, his or her attitude toward others was clinical, and any help he or she extended them was out of a sense of obligation. Now the individual is learning to draw strength from the reservoirs of love and compassion of the universe and to aid others out of faith.

This person will achieve growth and progress if he or she continues along the spiritual path, learning to tune in to cosmic awareness. The individual will use his or her feelings and intuitions to achieve growth, and will learn to sense the cosmic perfection that lies within.

chapter ten

RELATIONSHIPS
WITH THE DRAGON

The story goes round and round
From beginning to end
And the characters
Change faces and scenery
Appear and disappear
In the changing scripts of our existence.

—RUTH AHARONI

The Dragon plays a decisive role, not only in our understanding of the karmic process but also of karmic relationships. Contacts between the Dragon in one chart and planets in a second chart show relationships with souls from the past, lessons to be learned, and possibilities for growth by way of renewal of contact.

Through comparing two charts' planetary aspects or looking at planets' placements in houses, we come to understand what links two people. Yet when the Dragon enters the picture, we begin to understand the internal logic of this link, which initially appears not to have a logical foundation.

The nodes reveal the forces that caused the relationship to form, as well as the inner force that drives the relationship. This force is not the result of simple attraction, but rather is the result of a karmic force that is hard to resist and that must be expressed. The impression of the previous relationship is imprinted deep under the surface of the present relationship, and patterns and debts of the past play a key role.

As was explained in chapter 9, the Dragon's Tail represents the past; therefore, the person in whose chart a planet forms an aspect with the Tail in another chart will feel a magnetic pull to respond to the Tail individual. This pull is manifested strongly in conjunctions, as the planet individual feels a strong sense of indebtedness from a past incarnation toward the Tail individual, and it is extremely important to him or her to repay it. We have here unfinished business wherein energy must be invested in order to bring it to a resolution. This situation is manifested even more intensely in the event of a conjunction between the Ascendant in the first chart and the Dragon's Tail in the second.

In a situation such as the one described above, we have a relationship rooted in the past, as well as a pattern of voluntary subordination in which the Ascendant individual feels an overwhelming urge to give more and more to the Tail individual. To someone looking on from the sidelines, it may seem that the Ascendant individual is the sidekick of the Tail individual, yet the deeper reason for this behavior pattern is that both individuals sense a karmic debt that must be paid. Therefore, the Ascendant individual is actually giving voluntarily, and the Tail individual receives as if expected. Even though this relationship looks imbalanced, it is motivated by both individuals' common subconscious goal to behave thusly for the sake of balancing their shared karma.

Conjunctions of the Dragon's Tail with personal planets in a second chart show a relationship with a close soul; such a relationship is not necessarily an easy one. Despite the fact that on a subconscious level we may see a soul that truly loves us and offers us a chance to grow, the circumstances of such growth may be problematic. The lessons that must be learned from such a relationship are often unfathomable from the viewpoint of the present life; we must shift that viewpoint in order to examine them from a holistic point of view.

Aspects with the Dragon's Head do not in and of themselves indicate an obligatory relationship or debts from the past, yet the individuals involved may feel that they invest in each other for the sake of the future, so to speak. Such aspects do indicate a potential for a present relationship as well as one in a future incarnation whose foundation must be laid in this life.

SUN-TAIL

In this contact, the traces of a relationship from a previous incarnation are seen, in which the Sun individual was the strong and authoritative partner, and the Tail individual was always willing and available to submissively do the will of the Sun individual. In this incarnation, the Sun individual wants to continue to dominate the Tail individual. In a couple's relationship, for example, if the woman is represented by the Sun, she will dominate the man.

In any event, the Sun individual feels a strong connection with the Tail individual. On a subconscious level, he or she knows that in a past incarnation the Tail individual helped him or her out greatly, and in this life is taking the opportunity to repay this investment and the resulting accumulated debt. This is the reason that in this incarnation the Tail individual also takes for granted being on the receiving end of whatever the Sun individual is willing to give.

When the aspect between these two is harmonious, the Sun individual can help the Tail individual to overcome past fears that haunt him or her, and to develop willpower, individuality, and creativity. Yet if the aspect is disharmonious, the Tail individual will feel chained, restricted, and blocked by the relationship, because as explained above, with all of the giving in this incarnation, the Sun individual continues to dominate the Tail individual, preventing him or her from developing as a separate individual.

SUN-HEAD

The contact between these two, particularly the conjunction, indicates a new relationship between these two souls. In the event that other aspects show a karmic connection between them, then we are seeing a new aspect added to the old relationship.

There is no sense of indebtedness here; both individuals want the best for each other and invest positive energy in each other. Each awakens in the other self-expression, creative energy, trust, and respect. The Sun individual also awakens ambitions of personal growth in the Head individual. In the event that there is a karmic connection that requires healing energies, then this aspect offers the added value of karmic repair.

MOON-TAIL

This aspect indicates a strong emotional connection, particularly on the part of the Moon individual, who feels responsible for the emotional welfare of the Tail individual, supporting and protecting him or her. There is a suggestion here of an incarnational mother-child relationship, and the Tail individual may be emotionally dependent upon the Moon individual, radiating mental stability and emotional security onto him or her.

Therefore, particularly when disharmonious aspects are activated in this relationship, the Moon individual may occasionally feel exploited because he or she feels bound to sacrifice, while the Tail individual may reestablish a past pattern by becoming emotionally handicapped due to his or her habit of being dependent and displaying a constant need for emotional and mental support.

MOON-HEAD

In this aspect, there is more emotional reciprocity. These two provide each other with emotional support and enable each other to express feelings freely. If the aspect is disharmonious, a certain conflict may develop; yet their similar outlooks can serve as a durable foundation for a future relationship in the next life.

MERCURY-TAIL

This contact—typified by fluent communication and by transmission and reception of information—shows a strong mental affinity that began in a previous incarnation. These two were connected in the past as a teacher and a pupil or as siblings, or even as an employer and devoted trainee. In the present relationship, Mercury acts as a transmitter who wants to give as much as he or she can, and the Tail individual is the ultimate receptor.

When this aspect is disharmonious, the Mercury individual may go overboard in taking responsibility for the Tail individual, wishing to teach and educate him or her. The Mercury individual may be critical and nitpicking, possibly irritating the Tail individual. On the other hand, the Tail individual may sap the mental energies of the Mercury individual.

MERCURY-HEAD

This aspect shows that the foundation of the communication between these two was laid in this incarnation, and it is about to expand and develop. A refreshing exchange of ideas takes place between these two, with both on the same wavelength. When this aspect is harmonious, there is a superb level of understanding. In a disharmonious aspect, they will disagree, but even these disagreements will drive them to further mental growth.

VENUS-TAIL

The contact between these two shows that in a previous incarnation there was either an unfinished romance or a strong emotional tie between these two, yet circumstances did not allow the relationship to ripen and reach fulfillment. Therefore, relations ceased so that they could resume and bring the relationship to fruition in a later incarnation. The Venus individual feels a karmic obligation toward the Tail individual in various realms. Giving may be expressed romantically, emotionally, artistically, socially, or economically.

When this contact is harmonious, the Venus individual will offer his or her assistance out of respect for the Tail individual, and will try to bring him or her joy; in return, the Tail individual will derive benefit from the relationship, while he or she invests less.

A disharmonious contact may show the Tail individual to be demanding. While the Venus individual will respond to these demands due to a sense of obligation imprinted from a previous incarnation, the giving will be out of pressure, and the Tail individual may feel inferior and scorned.

VENUS-HEAD

This contact shows a fundamental attraction between these two, a two-way flow of feelings, and emotional involvement. There is a chance here for a romance to develop, if this is an option. This contact has a beneficial effect, and if it also has positive reinforcements from other planets, there is a chance that it will continue, bringing benefit to both sides.

MARS-TAIL

When this aspect is harmonious, the Mars individual pushes the Tail individual forward, enabling him or her to break free of past patterns and develop faith in him- or herself.

If this aspect is disharmonious, the relationship may be fraught with enmity. The Mars individual senses that the Tail individual binds him or her and saps his or her energy. On the one hand, the Mars individual is driven by the inner knowledge that he or she owes the Tail individual, but on the other hand, the Mars individual feels a lack of desire to fulfill his or her obligation, because he or she senses the blockages of the past exerting their influence. This aspect requires the Mars individual to behave patiently and swallow his or her pride; he or she must understand that stubbornness may cause a karmic debt to be dragged into the next incarnation.

MARS-HEAD

This is an aspect of stimulation, showing that the connection between these two is fiery. There is mutuality, openness, a two-way energy flow, and no heavy obligations. Even if these two do not see one another often, they trust the continuity of the relationship, as they have an unswerving foundation.

When the aspect is harmonious, there is healthy competition between these two, adding life to the relationship. Yet when it is disharmonious, it may show disagreements and quarrels. Each of them strokes his or her own ego, and if this is the case, they will find it difficult to cooperate and adapt to each other. Negative karma may build up that will be imprinted on the future karmic plan.

JUPITER-TAIL

When this aspect is harmonious, the Jupiter individual radiates good energy onto, is considerate of, and rewards the Tail individual materially and emotionally. The Tail individual takes all that he or she can wholeheartedly, and still the Jupiter individual simply continues spreading his or her goodness, because he or she is confident of his or her inexhaustible inner reserves.

If this aspect is disharmonious, the Jupiter individual may be irked by the Tail individual's real or perceived greed. The reason behind the Jupiter individual's generosity is the desire to repair mistakes of the past, to balance any karmic debts, and to establish cosmic justice. Yet because his or her style is didactic, he or she perceives the Tail individual's taking as negative karma, knowing that too much giving can go awry. Against this backdrop, conflicts may build, yet the lesson for both is a sense of proportion: the Jupiter individual must avoid squandering either material or emotional energy, and the Tail individual must avoid taking too much.

JUPITER-HEAD

This aspect shows mutual support, a similar philosophy of life, and communication for the purpose of advancing a joint goal. This contact is a catalyst for group, religious, or metaphysical activity, and is also good for studying together, whether as fellow students or as teacher and pupil. This contact sharpens and illuminates both individuals' worldviews and life directions.

SATURN-TAIL

A relationship affected by this contact is one that is hard to break away from. Each of these individuals brings to the relationship karmic baggage from which the other can learn meaningful lessons. The Saturn individual brings life experience and practical wisdom, serving as a teacher whose role is to transmit to the Tail individual his or her most important karmic lesson. The Saturn individual takes this job seriously, trying to help the Tail individual to tune in to past memories, because he or she knows that in this way the Tail individual can learn lessons for this life.

The Saturn individual recognizes the importance in this, yet the Tail individual is not necessarily comfortable with looking back, as it may be painful, and he or she tries to avoid this pain, turning his or her back on the past and diverting his or her eyes in a detached way toward the future. The aspects formed between the two charts will show whether the learning process is marred by conflict or whether it is more or less smooth.

SATURN-HEAD

This contact combines the practicality of Saturn with the innovativeness of the Head. When it is harmonious, these two can experience mutual growth that is slow yet steady. Yet when this contact is disharmonious, difficulties may surface that create conflict, because each tends to stick to his or her own attitudes, preventing a merging of the minds.

URANUS-TAIL

This contact shows an unconventional acquaintance in the incarnational past of these two, which ended suddenly and unexpectedly, leaving an imprint of the event on the subconscious of both individuals and threatening disquiet. In this life, too, this contact promises interest and uniqueness, yet not stability.

The Uranus individual encourages the Tail individual toward independence of mind, thereby causing him or her an emotional jolt; yet at the same time this shakeup may prevent the Tail individual from spinning his or her wheels, and help him or her to break free of old and binding patterns. The Uranus individual's karmic role here is to shatter behavior patterns in which the Tail individual is stuck, and if other aspects do not indicate a continuing relationship, then it is likely that the relationship will end when this job has been completed.

URANUS-HEAD

This relationship is more relaxed than the Uranus-Tail aspect, because nothing here points to a shared past that has left its imprint. At the same time, it is a strong and interesting connection that can have catalyzing implications for a future life. This aspect shows a shared, open approach and sense of liberation, which in the case of harmonious aspects will have a positive effect on the individuals. In the case of disharmonious aspects, the contact may be beset by nerves and unrest that can disrupt the building of a stable relationship.

NEPTUNE-TAIL

The Neptune individual brings to the life of the Tail individual a touch of the mystical. In the event that the contact is harmonious, it awakens in the Tail individual inspiration, developing the imagination and the intuition. Such a contact may indicate a relationship with a spiritual teacher from a previous incarnation that had a positive influence on the Tail individual.

A disharmonious contact between them may indicate a past relationship wherein negative use was made of mysticism; or the contact may awaken in the Tail individual memories of deceit or of being led astray by the Neptune individual, which left the Tail individual scarred.

Even if the Neptune individual is perceived by the Tail individual to be unrealistic or untrustworthy, the Tail individual will find it difficult to extricate him- or herself from the web of illusion, as the effect of the past still binds these two together.

NEPTUNE-HEAD

This contact can indicate cooperation in an esoteric realm. The Neptune individual can awaken the intuitive side of the Head individual, and together they may inspire each other's philosophical approach, transforming their worldview into one that is more universal. At its best, this contact can aid both in taking off for spiritual heights; yet in itself, it does not guarantee a permanent influence on their lives in the future.

PLUTO-TAIL

This relationship is intense, with a strong undercurrent that must burst forth sooner or later. There is a karmic debt here on the part of the Pluto individual, manifested by his or her domination of the Tail individual. The Pluto individual is an authority figure who has undertaken to protect the Tail individual, yet he or she actually monopolizes him or her. If the contact is disharmonious, the Pluto individual may be coercive, possessive, or jealous, and if the Tail individual tries to break away, it may cause an outburst that acts as a volcanic eruption on the entire relationship.

When the contact is harmonious, the Pluto individual's power provides the Tail with individual protection and a sense of security; indeed, the Tail individual enjoys the patronage of the Pluto individual's ennobling power. The Pluto individual strengthens the Tail individual's inner powers, stimulating his or her insight so that the Pluto individual may pay his or her karmic debt and thus free the Tail individual to go his or her way.

PLUTO-HEAD

This is a direct, intense, and purposeful contact. Both individuals have the will to uncover their innermost depths, and this contact enables them both to do so thoroughly, and thus to see things with clarity.

A disharmonious contact may trigger a destructive invasiveness, particularly from the Pluto side, and the relationship may be irksome. If the contact is harmonious, it will stimulate, catalyze, and inspire optimism, enabling both individuals to complete processes of transformation.

CHAPTER ELEVEN

KARMIC COUPLES
AND COSMIC COUPLES

You were born together, and together
you shall be forever more.
You shall be together when the white wings
of death scatter your days.
Ay, you shall be together even in the
silent memory of God.

—"THE MARRIAGE" FROM *The Prophet* BY KAHLIL GIBRAN

She sounded excited as she contacted me to make an appointment for past-life regression therapy: "I must find out about a past incarnation in which we met. It's clear to
me that this man and I knew each other in the past. He also feels it, despite the fact that
he considers it just a metaphor. He's rational and skeptical about this stuff . . ." Yet just a
month after they met, Aharon accompanied Ada (fictitious names) to her appointment
with me, displaying the consideration and tolerance characteristic of a Libra; he had no
idea how much he typified his sign.

Ada, a Gemini with its typical disquiet and rational nature, did not easily enter the
suggestible state necessary for regression. Yet gradually her obstinate rational brain was
silenced, and Ada's body and consciousness entered a state of deep relaxation. She began
talking in a trance about an incarnation that she had experienced.

In this session, she regressed to two past lives. The first was not relevant to the purpose of her coming. In the second half of the session she found herself in a former life in Europe at the end of the nineteenth century and the beginning of the twentieth century.

She experienced being a young woman, and she identified her current partner as having been her partner at that time. She began to describe certain events, but at a certain stage, the flow of information suddenly stopped.

I brought her back to the present, and our session ended. Since every session is recorded, we were able to listen to the cassette later on and identify the event that stopped her from continuing. It had been a scene in which she had witnessed her own funeral.

I followed Ada's regression session with a channeled meditation, and thus discovered the missing details of Ada's life in her last incarnation:

> She was born in Vienna to a respected family. Her name was Helen. From a young age, she displayed impressive writing talent, and her ambition was to be a writer. At age eighteen, she met the love of her life, and they got engaged. However, he had yet to find a profession, so he went to Berlin to study. Not long after he left for Berlin, she became ill with tuberculosis and was hospitalized in a sanatorium. There she continued to write until her death shortly before her nineteenth birthday. Her fiancé returned to Vienna after she died, and suffered anguish at not having been at her side during her illness.

At the end of the channeling session, I received her birth date in that incarnation, as well as the exact time of her birth and the date of her death. As I drew her birth chart, I got goosebumps.

About half of the planets in "Helen's" chart populated her twelfth house, which represents closed places and hospitals. Half of the planets, as well as the Ascendant, were placed in Gemini, Ada's Sun sign in her present life.

Gemini is a sign associated with writing skills, and healthwise it is associated with lung ailments. Quite interesting details were revealed to me after I consulted astrologer Charles Carter's *Encyclopaedia of Psychological Astrology*. Carter identifies degree 6 in Gemini as indicating the possibility of a lung ailment, and this was the degree of Helen's Sun in that incarnation.

Carter points out that degrees indicating an extraordinary sensitivity to "consumption" (tuberculosis) are those adjacent to 28° in the mutable signs. Of course, Mercury, the ruler

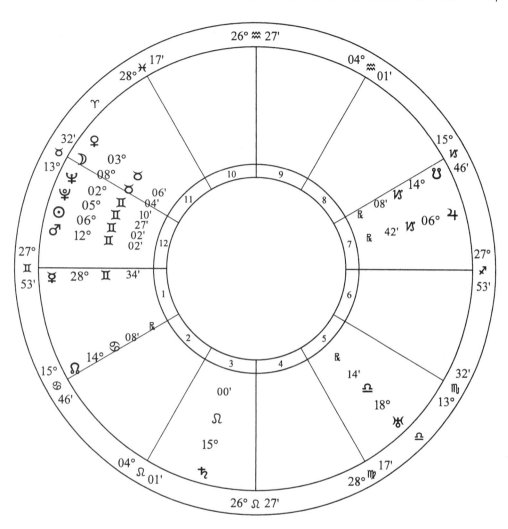

Figure 11—Ada's Chart in a Previous Life as Helen

May 27, 1889 / 5:35 a.m. Local Mean Time / Vienna, Austria

of Helen's Ascendant, was located at 28° Gemini in her first house, and the Ascendant degree that opened her first house (the first house represents the person's health condition) was 27°53' Gemini (figure 11).

Since she had died at an early age, leaving her ambition to be a writer unrealized, and because she also died before her marriage, Helen's soul returned to a new existence after only a short time. Souls that leave the world before satisfying their longings hurry to be re-embodied on Earth in order to continue the flow and to realize their purpose.

In this life, Ada married young, divorced a few years later, and for thirty years chose not to remarry. Aquarius, which opens her present seventh house (the marriage house), indicates this choice. She nurtured her career and social life and became a successful journalist and author.

In both Ada's charts (the one from this life and the one from her former life), we see that the unrealized planets in the earlier chart lie in the background of the tenth house in her present chart, acting as a catalyst behind the scenes that drove her to realize her career aspirations, enabling her to acquire the fame and prestige that were "overdue" in this life.

The area of career in the chart of Ada's present life shows other reinforcing elements, such as the fact that her former Moon sign (Taurus) becomes a tenth-house sign in her present chart, and it is also the sign of the Sun's ruler, Mercury, which is placed in the tenth house (figure 12). The Sun itself, as well as Venus, the ruler of the tenth, are in Gemini, the sign associated with writing and communication.

Ada met Aharon at a social gathering that strongly resembled an event that she had experienced in her regression session. At the time that he met Ada, Aharon had been a widower for two years, and was involved in a serious relationship with another woman. The two fell in love instantly, with Aharon abandoning his other relationship. After they began dating, Ada learned that Aharon had cared for his wife for many years during an extended illness. This devotion was a way of balancing his karmic debt: Because in his former life he had not been at his love's side as she lay in her sick bed, this time around he chose a relationship wherein he would have to care for a sick wife until her death.

With Ada, who had been his lover in their past life, Aharon chose to continue the love that had held so much promise and had been cut off in its youth. Shortly after meeting Ada in this life, he proposed to her, and they moved in together. A year and a half after their meeting, the two married, both of them past age sixty. They now live like youngsters, enjoying each other in day-to-day life and traveling the world together.

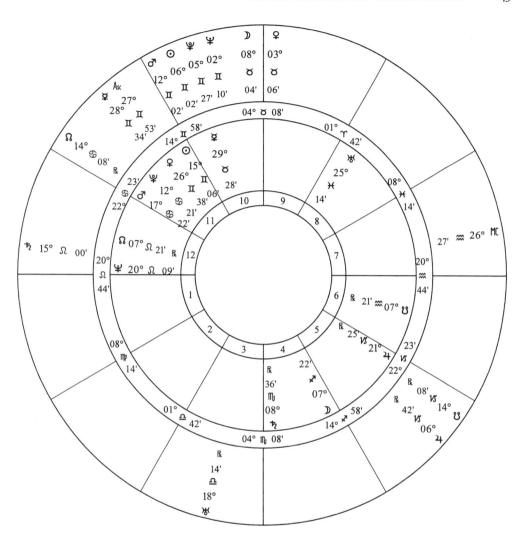

Figure 12—The Combined Charts of Ada and Helen

Inner Ring: Ada
June 6, 1925 / 9:30 a.m. Standard Time / Time Zone: 1 hour East / Kiel, Germany

Outer Ring: Helen
May 27, 1889 / 5:35 a.m. Local Mean Time / Vienna, Austria

Thus, a young couple that was engaged at the beginning of the twentieth century returned and was reunited by the power of love, fully realizing their karmic couple-hood at the end of the twentieth century, nearly ninety years later.

Ada and Aharon's synastry includes many karmic conjunctions (figure 13). The magnetic karmic attraction between these two partners is revealed by the exact conjunction between his Pluto and her Mars. This intensive planetary contact adds fire, thrills, and desire to the relationship. Because this conjunction lies in the eleventh house, it shows that there is also a deep friendship between them.

The physical attraction is also revealed in the exact conjunction between her Uranus and his Jupiter in the eighth house. Uranus's involvement in karmic relations indicates a relationship that was cut off suddenly, and the location of the planetary conjunction in the eighth house, the house of death, suggests the reason for the former relationship's end. This conjunction, as well as the location of his Dragon's Tail, which falls in her fifth house, reveal that there was a love relationship between these partners in a former incarnation that was to be reestablished in this incarnation. In Aharon's chart, Jupiter rules his seventh house (the marriage house). In Ada's chart, Uranus rules her seventh. Thus, both rulers of both their marriage houses have united in order to realize the relationship.

The conjunction of Ada's Sun with Aharon's Dragon's Head shows a new shared life in this incarnation, and both partners wish to benefit one another and to invest positive energy in each other, thereby creating mutual trust and respect. This aspect has the added value of repair for relationships begun in a previous life that need beneficial energy.

Other conjunctions that reveal a past relationship intended for ultimate realization and mutual commitment include a conjunction that falls in Ada's fourth house (the family house) between Saturn, the ruler of her marriage house, and Mercury, the ruler of Aharon's chart, as well as a conjunction between Aharon's Saturn and Ada's Moon, which also falls in her fourth house.

The harmony between these two partners is above all revealed in the Grand Trines formed between their two charts. A trine aspect is formed between their Suns, and both their Suns and Ada's seventh-house cusp form a Grand Trine. In addition, the conjunction of Ada's Venus with Aharon's Dragon's Head forms harmonious trines with Aharon's Sun and Mars and with Ada's seventh-house cusp.

The most prominent element in this combined chart is fire, showing the desire that motivated their coming together, and also the spontaneity of their relationship. In this life,

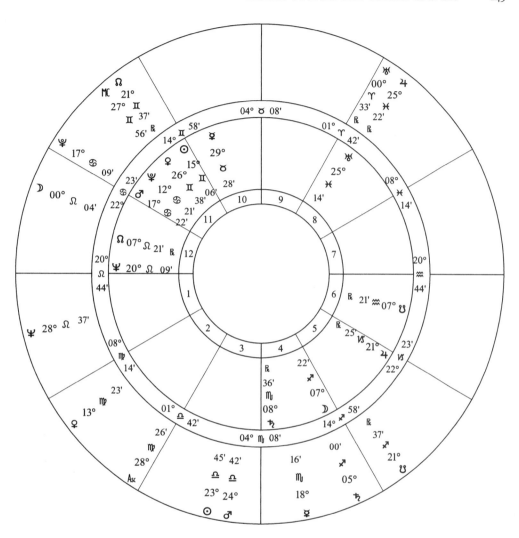

Figure 13—The Combined Charts of Ada and Aharon

Inner Ring: Ada
June 6, 1925 / 9:30 a.m. Standard Time / Time Zone: 1 hour East / Kiel, Germany

Outer Ring: Aharon
October 18, 1927 / 4:15 a.m. Standard Time / Time Zone: 1 hour East / Berlin, Germany

they are both resolved to erase the limitations of the past that prevented their uniting, and they both place an emphasis on intensive, shared enjoyable activity and on "pushing the boundaries" of their present life.

KARMIC COUPLEHOOD

The charts just described show to what extent every detail in our former lives has significance vis-à-vis our total understanding of our present lives. The balancing of both an individual's and a couple's karma plays itself out in various ways, at times bizarrely, and the soul's creativity is manifested in countless variations and scenarios.

Both the regression technique and astrological charts are paths to self-awareness. A relationship, too, can act as a bridge to our inner selves, a path along which we can discover and learn more about ourselves.

When an individual lives within him- or herself, he or she becomes enclosed within borders, and in the best-case scenario, learns to live in inner harmony. When another "character" wanders onto the stage and joins the drama, the rules of the game change; the interaction between them changes the script being played out, and bonds are created, the aim of whose fulfillment is to cultivate a relationship. However, occasionally these ties disturb the balance; the objective of karmic couplehood is to restore this balance, to achieve harmony, and to realize their shared sense of coming together.

When an individual opens him- or herself to an encounter with another, he or she summons up experiences that can aid him or her in coping with karmic load that must be unloaded, and with karmic problems whose solutions can be expedited by an encounter with another. Problematic karmic relationships provide fuel for personal development. We can use this fuel in a mature, correct, and positive way, or alternatively we can spill it carelessly so that it ignites a fire that emits thick black smoke that can block our learning capacity.

Remember, astrologically speaking, human relationships are represented by relationships between the planets in the partners' charts. An aspect between planets represents the connection between the planets' energy fields, i.e., between the energy fields of the active souls, such that we can learn about the nature of the relationship by looking at the aspects formed between the planets in one partner's chart and those in the other's. We can also learn about the relationship by looking at where the planets of each partner fall in the other partner's chart.

The nature of a relationship also depends upon the manner in which the partners express the planetary energy. When we express the positive facet of a planet, we attract a loving karmic response and the capacity to realize the relationship from a place of joy and pleasure. On the other hand, if we express a planet's negative facet, we attract negative counter-energy that evokes pain and can be destructive.

When, in comparing two charts, a multiplicity of harmonious aspects between the planets of the two active souls is revealed, and there are few disharmonious aspects, it shows that the relationship is *too* relaxed, and karmic friction that stimulates and piques the relationship is missing. The dynamic aspects are those that provide the incentive and the stimulus that partners need in order to grow and develop self-awareness, and to learn to appreciate the unique identity of the other.

When partners must balance their shared karma, the disharmonious aspects show on the one hand karma that was not balanced in a former life, and on the other hand they show the challenge that lies before the couple. These disharmonious aspects actually represent opportunities for learning, and to the extent that the right effort is made, they act as a guarantee of future compensation.

Then again, a multiplicity of disharmonious aspects shows difficulties and obstacles, stress and conflict, and even possibly depression, disloyalty, or manipulation that must be overcome. This disharmony can go on for years, until the partners learn to cut corners, to dull the sting, and to ultimately achieve the balance and harmony of the relationship. Occasionally, the personalities of the partners are so dissimilar and the tension is so thick that no amount of effort can enable them to achieve harmony, and there is really no possibility of their compatibility.

Balance between the flowing and dynamic aspects is the key to a fulfilling relationship, thus ensuring the achievement of karmic balance. The oppositions cause the partners to be attracted to each other, the conjunctions provide the unifying "glue," the harmonious aspects ensure the sweet moments of a shared life, and the dynamic aspects embody the challenges in the relationship.

In comparing the charts of partners who are **matched souls**, we see a fundamental harmony between the planetary energies. Grand Trines are typical of such a relationship. The dynamic aspects between two charts do not cloud the connection, but rather act as factors that aid in perfecting the karmic balance between the partners.

The combined chart of two partners who are **twin souls** show many conjunctions of planets in the same sign. We do not necessarily see conjunctions between the two partners'

Suns. There may be conjunctions between the Sun and the Moon, between the Sun and the Ascendant, between the ruler of the Ascendent and the Sun, between the rulers of both charts, or between significant planets in one chart and those in the other.

Such conjunctions, which show the *similarity* between these souls, do not in every case show *harmony* between them. Disharmonious aspects that appear in each of their charts can appear in a comparison of the two charts in a multiple emphasis, and thus the disharmony obtains reinforcement and intensifies. Therefore, when there is a multiplicity of disharmonious aspects, each partner is in conflict not only with him- or herself, but also with the other. The tension can proliferate, and the interaction and learning between these partners can become quite complicated. The success of such a relationship depends on the inner work that each partner does. When each learns to balance the opposing forces within, then the relationship between twin souls can be a pleasurable one of togetherness and unity.

The attraction between karmic partners is symbolized by the aspects between inner planets in one partner's chart and outer planets in the other's chart. Harmonious aspects between inner planets indicate a good present-life relationship, yet not necessarily a karmic relationship from the past. Only when there is involvement of outer planets with significant inner planets do we see a continuous karmic connection.

A conjunction of outer planets of one chart with angular cusps (the first, fourth, seventh, and tenth houses) of the other chart, or the location of the outer planets in one chart in the angular houses of the other chart, indicates a karmic relationship between the partners. The Ascendant/Descendant axis is always involved in a significant relationship.[1]

Another factor characteristic of karmic couplehood is a *T-Square* formed between planets of both charts in which the Dragon is involved.

In the comparison of Ada's and Aharon's charts in figure 13, Uranus, which rules Ada's marriage house, is at the apex of a T-Square. It forms a square aspect with her Venus and Sun, and with Aharon's Dragon's Head and Tail. Aharon's Tail in turn forms oppositions to Ada's Venus and Sun, which are both conjunct Aharon's Dragon's Head (see figure 14).

COSMIC COUPLEHOOD

The relationship between **cosmic partners** is one in which both similarities and differences are closely combined. The conjunction shows at which points the two souls "kiss," and the opposition shows where they complete one another.

---

1. A conjunction with a house cusp can be taken into account only in precise charts that have undergone mathematical correction.

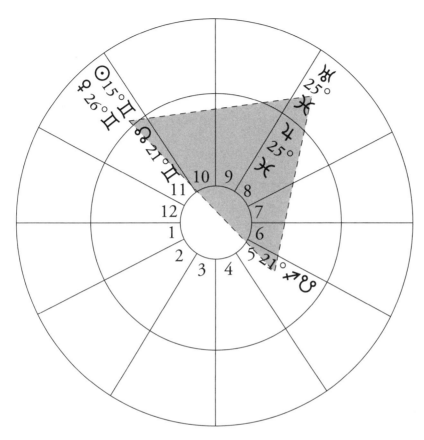

Figure 14—The Karmic T-Square

The lines of similarity between the partners are symbolized by the conjunctions between their inner planets; the tight karmic connection is symbolized by many karmic conjunctions, i.e., conjunctions between inner planets and outer planets; and the karmic attraction and the completions of the opposites are symbolized by the oppositions. The uniqueness of the synastry of cosmic couples is manifested in the two charts being interwoven, with nearly all of the planets therein interlaced.

This tight weave includes close conjunctions between planets in one chart with angular cusps in the other chart, particularly with the Ascendant/Descendant axis, and it includes one or more configurations of the Grand Cross, in which one of the Dragons is involved.

In complementary charts, the Dragon's Tail in one chart has a distinguishable influence on the other chart. In such a case the Tail falls in one of the angular houses; in conjunction to a cusp of an angular house; and/or in conjunction with inner planets or with the

Ascendant in the other's chart. A conjunction between the Dragon's Tail and Saturn is significant, and strongly links the karmic connection between the two souls.

Another factor that must appear in the synastry of two completing souls is that the horizon axes in both charts must be in conjunction or create a Grand Cross, i.e., both Ascendants must be conjunct, in opposition, or in a square aspect; hence, the horizon axes in both charts must open in the same quadruplicity. Thus the ascending and descending signs in both charts will be either cardinal, fixed, or mutable.

When, in addition to these characteristics, the charts obtain positive planetary influences of harmonious aspects, or, when in the synastry there are Grand Trines, and there is balance between the flowing and dynamic aspects, then cosmic couplehood is not only completing but perfected.

The combined charts of Edgar Cayce and his secretary, Gladys Davis, are an excellent example of the strong astrological connection between cosmic couples (figures 15A and 15B).

The horizon axes in both charts open in the fixed signs, or "chariot signs" (see page 78), in almost the same degree, and both these cusps together form a fixed Grand Cross. This cross shows the strong karmic connection between Davis and Cayce, which began many incarnations ago. In Cayce's soul readings that he performed in a full trance, in which he spoke of the cosmic connection between them, he said:

> We find these, as in the present earth's plane, have had many experiences together and their soul and spirit are well-knit, and must of necessity present each that they may be one. . . . [I]n the beginning . . . these two . . . were as one in mind, soul, spirit, body; and in the first earth's plane [Atlantis] . . . when . . . the earth's indwelling of man was both male and female in one. . . .
>
> [In Atlantis] we find then the separation of the body. For the desire of the flesh being to give of self in bodily form to the other, it brought the separating of the spirit and soul from the carnal forces . . . (from Edgar Cayce reading 286–8, © The Edgar Cayce Foundation)
>
> The lives of each have ever been bound in the other's life, and the conditions as exist are only the outgrowth of endeavor in the earth plane. They, the relations in the present, should be the ever-innate affection as is necessary in the lives of each, for the satisfying not of the earthly forces, but of the soul and spirit which find manifestation in material affection. Let that affection be such as gives of self to each, in no uncertain terms or physical manner, but ever in the answering of each desire toward the other in the way that gives self's affection. That is, the outward manifestations

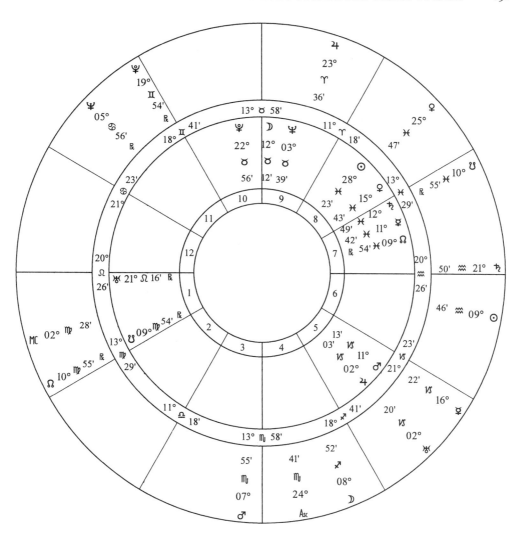

Figure 15A—The Combined Charts of Edgar Cayce and Gladys Davis

Inner Ring: Edgar Cayce
March 18, 1877 / 3:00 p.m. Local Mean Time / Hopkinsville, Kentucky

Outer Ring: Gladys Davis
January 30, 1905 / 1:30 a.m. Central Standard Time / Centerville, Alabama

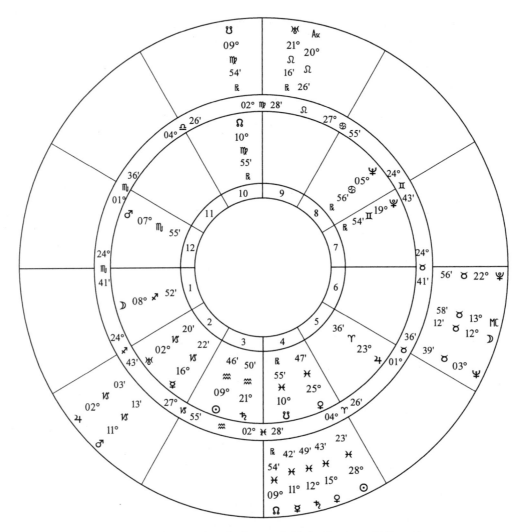

Figure 15B—The Combined Charts of Gladys Davis and Edgar Cayce

Inner Ring: Gladys Davis
January 30, 1905 / 1:30 a.m. Central Standard Time / Centerville, Alabama

Outer Ring; Edgar Cayce
March 18, 1877 / 3:00 p.m. Local Mean Time / Hopkinsville, Kentucky

of the inward desires of the heart and soul, which find in each the answering chord in the other's affection that will never, never, never be found in any other. . . . (from Edgar Cayce reading 294–9)

According to records made based on Cayce's readings while in the trance, Davis had been his wife, daughter, and mother in various incarnations. Indeed, Davis's fourth house is populated by Cayce's planets, showing the multi-incarnation family connection between them.

Their karmic connection is also revealed in all the conjunctions between their charts. There is a conjunction between Davis's Dragon's Tail and all of the planets in Cayce's seventh house, including his Saturn. His Sun conjoins Davis's Venus, which rules her marriage house. Cayce's Pluto is located exactly in Davis's seventh-house degree, and Davis's Saturn conjoins Cayce's seventh-house cusp. The conjunction of Saturn from one chart with one of the cusps of the angular houses of the other chart always shows a strong element of karmic obligation.

Other significant conjunctions between the charts include close conjunctions between Cayce's Dragon's Head and Davis's Dragon's Tail, and between Davis's Dragon's Head and Cayce's Dragon's Tail. These conjunctions enable both souls to reap the benefit of the concentrated energy of the encounters between Heads and Tails. Such an encounter reinforces the ability of each partner to learn karmic lessons in the most fruitful and productive way, and to invest effectively in a shared karmic goal for which they have reached this world.

The encounter of the Dragons forms two conjunctions and two oppositions, which appear in Davis's chart in her fourth and tenth houses, and in Cayce's chart in his first and seventh houses. This is a unique karmic crossroads encounter that shows that both their lives are intertwined in the strongest possible way.

Conjunctions between Heads and Tails in chart comparisons show that both partners knew one another in a former incarnation, and will continue their acquaintance in this incarnation, yet they will not be able to consummate their relationship due to karmic circumstances.

In the case of Cayce and Davis, despite their being cosmic partners, they could not fulfill a marriage relationship. The sexual attraction between them, which was not consummated in this incarnation, manifested in oppositions between her Mars and his Moon. In both their charts, these planets are associated with the twelfth house, the house that represents the subconscious.

While Davis's Pluto and Moon are not part of the weave of conjunctions and oppositions, they are part of the karmic Grand Cross with the Dragons, and form dynamic aspects with Cayce's planets, which are located in Pisces. Pluto, which rules Davis's chart, falls in Cayce's tenth house, at the threshold of the eleventh. This shows that Davis devoted her life to a common social and spiritual goal that she and Cayce had both set for themselves. In addition, Davis permitted herself to fulfill her own desire for marriage only after the Cayces' deaths in 1945, three months apart.

The spiritual connection between Davis and Cayce is also revealed in the planetary influence over both their ninth houses. Davis's Jupiter falls in Cayce's ninth house, emphasizing the fact that she contributed her spiritual talents to disseminating Cayce's knowledge derived from channeling, and that she was an active partner in his knowledge gathering. Furthermore, Davis's Jupiter forms harmonious aspects with the conjunction of Cayce's Uranus and Ascendant. Both Cayce's Ascendant and his Uranus fall in Davis's ninth house, thereby endowing it with inspiration.

The special relationship between these three souls, revealed in our time as Edgar Cayce, his wife, Gertrude, and his secretary, Gladys Davis, received special attention in Cayce's spiritual readings. Despite the fact that his readings pointed to a cosmic relationship between himself and Davis, this relationship could not be consummated, as in this incarnation Cayce's soul was put to a test. It was incumbent upon him to balance previous incarnations during which he had given in to lust, so that in this incarnation he was devoted to the sanctity of marriage and remained faithful to his wife.

Besides the personal testimony that Davis gave regarding her warm relationship with Gertrude Cayce, those who knew both women well described their relationship as resembling a mother-daughter bond. In this incarnation, all three came back to have a three-way interaction in order to heal the pain of separation that they experienced in previous incarnations. In their shared lives in ancient Egypt, Davis was the Cayces' daughter, but circumstances cut her off from them. In this life, circumstances (which, as we know, are never coincidental) sent Davis "back" to the Cayces when she was nineteen years old, and in the ensuing two decades, she was an integral part of their family, with the Cayces acting as surrogate parents.

In their twentieth-century incarnation, all three came together to balance both their individual and family karma, together with the fulfillment of their karmic goal on behalf of which they shared an incarnation: solving health and personal problems, raising spiritual consciousness, and disseminating the abundance of knowledge channeled by Cayce, an endeavor that continues even today, reaching all over the globe.

chapter tweLve

SPIRITUAL ATTRACTION

. . . when I found him whom my soul loveth,
I held him, and would not let him go . . .
Draw me, we will run after thee . . .

—Song of Songs 3:4, 1:4

To attract a worthy partner, you yourself must feel worthy. A person attracts those who are compatible with his or her vibrations and energies, as well as his or her beliefs about him- or herself. We've already said that a person is a product of his or her consciousness. Therefore, it is incumbent upon the individual to "scrub and clean the chambers of his or her consciousness" until he or she is ready to receive the desired guest. If the preparatory work is not done, then the uninvited guest will simply "drop in," instead of the invited one. This preparatory work can be done through the *chakras*, or the astral energy system that powers the physical body.

Of course, a person is not merely a physical body. Individuals who identify themselves only with their physical being do themselves an injustice in ignoring their most valuable asset: the soul. In relating only to the physical level of the body, we shortchange our subtler bodies, whose nurturing is no less important than the nurturing of our physical body.

According to yoga, a person has three bodies comprised of five sheaths, or *koshas* (referred to as "bodies" in today's literature), which are the vehicles of the soul in which it functions. Thus these bodies are linked and affect each other.

The **physical body**, or the one "worn" as a garment for the purpose of the present journey through the world—or the present incarnation—is the material body that perishes at death. The sheath that comprises it is the physical sheath (figure 16).

The **astral body** is linked by a gossamer thread to the physical body. During deep sleep, the astral body can exit and hover over the physical body. It can even do so at our will and make astral journeys. Only at the moment of death is the thread linking the two bodies cut, and the astral body cannot return to unite with the physical body.

The astral body is itself comprised of three sheaths. The first, known as the *vital sheath*, or the *etheric double*, is comprised of material more delicate than that of the physical body, yet whose form is very similar to that of the physical body. It is possible to see the etheric double leave the physical body at the moment of death, and it is the one that we call a "ghost." The vital sheath survives for a while after death, and souls that are attached to the physical world and refuse to leave it and pass on to the astral world continue to function in this sheath in order to continue experiencing the physical world.

The other sheaths of the astral body are the *emotional sheath* and the *intellectual sheath*, which contain the feelings, beliefs, and opinions that the person acquired during his or her life, and which the person continues to carry with him or her in the transition to the astral world.

The **causal body**, also called the *spiritual body*, contains one sheath: the **bliss sheath**. This is the most delicate body of all, and it develops along with the person's spiritual growth. It is through this sheath that the person experiences happiness, contentment, and serenity, and can reach the supreme peace, achieved through spiritual experiences.

The chakras are the energy centers in the etheric body. There are many chakras all over the body, but the seven main chakras are located along the body's vertical axis (figure 17). These chakras are linked to specific nerve ganglia, glands, and organs in the physical body, yet they also relate to human qualities and behaviors. The order of the chakras' locations marks a progressive path on a journey of self-discovery, along which a person can travel and achieve optimal physical health and full realization of his or her human potential.

In terms of human development, the chakras represent the path from childhood to adulthood, to maturity. From a psychological standpoint, the first part of life is characterized by the consolidation of the ego, the first steps away from the family unit, and the shaping of the outward-directed personality. The second part of life is characterized by a turning inward, the development of self-awareness, the search for meaning, and understanding one's connection with the deeper layers of the personality.

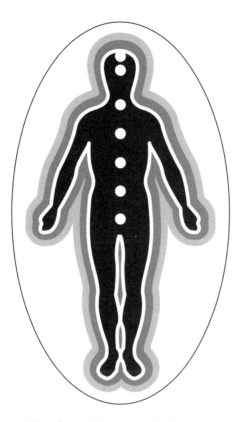

Figure 16—The Physical Body and the Four Energy Bodies

Within each of us is the constant striving for unity and harmony. This striving runs counter to the experiences of the external reality, which contain multiplicity and duality, conflicts and divisiveness. The roots of the yearning for unity lie in the experience of harmony, which the soul experienced at the moment of its dwelling in pure, total existence. The soul knows that the unity, which harmoniously blends the opposing forces, lies beyond the multiplicity existing in the mind.

When we focus during meditation on our chakras, we create an energetic link between ourselves, or the *microcosmos*, and the universe, or the *macrocosmos*. This link is made possible because beyond the chakras in our bodies are others outside the body that together form an entire energetic system. Experiencing unity and harmony is the goal of the work on the chakras; when each of us achieves this experience in our individual body, we can also achieve it in our relationships and thus experience fully the unity of the cosmos.

The various mystical teachings emphasize the need to build pure vessels, in which the divine light can be embodied. Abundant cosmic light is available to anyone who makes him- or herself a vessel worthy of containing abundance, and the chakras are a network of vessels that can be developed.

The meaning of the Sanskrit word *chakra* is "wheel"; indeed, chakras are the wheels of life leading to enlightenment and unity. The chakras vibrate in a rotating direction that creates a sort of whirlpool, similar to the electric action in a battery. Each chakra is a center of turbulence that acts on a different frequency and generates a different reverberation. The first center acts on the lowest frequency and creates the densest energetic reverberation, and the last center creates the highest-pitched energetic reverberation.

We can think of the chakras as lotus flowers, because they open and close as do the petals of a flower, and they are arranged along the astral spinal cord, which serves as their stem. When a chakra is not active, it is closed, and the life force cannot flow through it. When it is too active, it draws a quantity of energy at the expense of the rest of the chakras. In any case, an imbalance is created that must be corrected. A chakra that is balanced and functions properly acts on its regular frequency. When it does not, it is either overworking or underworking. A person usually functions with the chakras that are most developed in him or her. Therefore, we should work on the chakras that are the least developed, thereby achieving balance.

A chakra is depicted as a mandala, a universal symbol made up of a circle with a square and a triangle inside it. The symmetrical shapes symbolize perfection and harmony; the mandala as a whole is a symbol of uniting opposites, and its centerpoint symbolizes the self. In addition, each chakra is associated with a color based on the colors of the spectrum. Concentrating on each chakra, and the color associated with it, is one way to release blockages and achieve balance. Muscial notes and mantras, too, create vibrations that affect the chakras and balance them.

The chakras are connected to each other, and in order to develop the spiritual powers that lie within the upper chakras, we must work on opening the blockages in the lower chakras. We do so because in order to reach high levels of inner joy and pure love for self and others, we must deal in the correct way with lower urges and feelings. By opening blockages and balancing the chakra system, we experience the process of liberation from limitations.

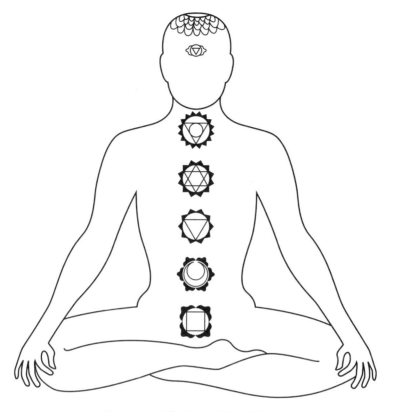

Figure 17—The Seven Main Chakras

Work on the chakras is a lifelong process, and certain exercises whose purpose is to elevate the *kundalini*, or latent cosmic force that lies at the base of the chakra system, must be performed *only* under the direct supervision of a specialist teacher. This chapter presents simple exercises for activating the chakras toward their balance. These exercises are quite effective and can be practiced safely.

When a person functions in a balanced way, using all of his or her energy centers, his or her ability to function fully in all areas of life is optimal, and he or she has the option of expanding the limits of his or her potential. This person will become more able to take control of his or her life and shape it according to his or her will. It will be within the individual's power to create successful life circumstances, and to attract the right partner with whom he or she can balance both personal and couple karma.

THE CHAKRA SYSTEM

The first chakra is the **root chakra**, or *Muladhara*. The root chakra is the energy center at the base of the spine, and the color related to it is red, the first color of the spectrum. The Muladhara represents the element of earth and the instinctual level. It is depicted in the shape of a circle with four lotus petals, and inside of that, a square. The square and the number 4 represent material, foundation, solidity, and stability; this chakra is in charge of the understanding of the physical dimension, acquiring basic needs, and survival ability. The gland connected with the Muladhara is the adrenal gland.

When this chakra is functioning properly, the person is activated soundly in a physical sense and "has both feet on the ground." The individual feels strong and content with what he or she has, with no fear of material lack. He or she is tuned in a healthy and balanced way to his or her childhood, past, family, and homeland.

Flawed and imbalanced functioning of a chakra can be manifested in two ways: blockages or leakages. A person whose Muladhara is imbalanced will attract people with problems connected to the material dimension. If this chakra is blocked, the individual will attract people who are rigid like him- or herself, with whom he or she is not able to experience spontaneous energetic flow. These people will determine the individual's stingy approach to life. If this chakra is overactive, the person will attract materialists and parasites who will exploit his or her extravagance, live at his or her expense, and sap his or her material and physical resources.

Meditation on the root chakra strengthens one's feelings of belonging and one's connections with one's roots. It also brings one closer to the Earth and nature, reinforces instinctual responses, and increases vitality, security, and stability. This meditation will raise the self-image, the power to attract abundance and use it wisely, and enables one to go out confidently into the world and succeed in day-to-day life.

The second chakra, the **sacral chakra**, or *Svadhisthana*, is related to the genitals, and it shares the responsibility for survival of the race with the root chakra below it. Svadhisthana is located just above the genitalia, under the navel, and is related to the sex glands, or gonads.

Svadhisthana is depicted as a circle around a crescent facing upward, surrounded by six lotus petals. The number 6 represents balance, love, and harmony. The color associated with Svadhisthana is orange, which also represents balance and empathy. This chakra is in charge of creating interpersonal connections and experiencing the spontaneous flow of give-and-take. The sacral chakra's element is water, and it controls sensuality and creativity.

When Svadhisthana is balanced, the person attracts partners with whom he or she will have not only gratifying sexual experiences, but also a high level of emotional closeness. This person will be healthy and vital in this region, and his or her sexual functioning is sound. Fears and conflicts with a sexual background block this chakra and sexual energy, which can trigger neurotic behavior on one level or another. On the one hand, this chakra's overfunctioning may be manifested in promiscuity; on the other hand, its underfunctioning may be manifested in sexual inhibition or dysfunction. Either way, disruption of the sound functioning of this chakra can cause imbalance throughout the system.

Meditation on this center strengthens sexual vitality, balances the expression of passion, and increases creative powers. Concentration on the color orange in the context of this center also opens up our consideration of others, making us more congenial and sensitive to them.

The next chakra is the **solar plexus**, or *Manipura*. It is located in the midriff, above the navel. Manipura's element is fire, and the gland related to it is the pancreas. It is depicted as a mandala surrounding a triangle around which are ten lotus petals. The number 10 represents supremacy, self-worth, capacity for action, willpower, and self-control. Likewise, Manipura is the center of power, control, and will. When this chakra is balanced and functioning soundly, our gut responses are on the mark, and can guide us through our everyday activities.

The color associated with Manipura is yellow, which among others represents mental capacity, through which we control our emotions. When we lose control—become overexcited or frightened, for instance—we "leak" energy that is concentrated in this chakra, and as a result feel helpless and drained, so much so that we feel a "pit" in this region. In contrast, when we behave domineeringly, aggressively, or angrily, we cause the overfunctioning of this chakra and its consequent blockage.

Meditating on the solar plexus chakra enables activation of power in a balanced way; reinforces physical and mental vitality; improves self-control, emotional control, and awareness; and reduces or eliminates fears, nervousness, and worry. Strengthening this chakra is also "insurance" against others' controlling us, as our will is activated to guard our interests and achieve our goals.

The **heart chakra**, or *Anahata*, is the central chakra that serves as a bridge between the lower and upper chakras. The color associated with Anahata is green, a calming and balancing color, and the middle color in the spectrum. Achieving balance is indeed one function of this chakra. Anahata is depicted as a mandala in whose center is a six-pointed star around which are twelve lotus petals. The number 12 symbolizes emotional depth, tranquility, and the capacity for closeness; numerologically, the sum of 1 and 2 is 3, the number symbolizing integration, balance, and wholeness. Anahata's element is air, which has no shape or boundaries and is the least tangible of the four elements. These properties are analogous to those of love, the natural function of the heart chakra.

The heart chakra is related to the thymus gland, which is in charge of the immune system, and as we know, love strengthens the immune system and our capacity to overcome illness, as testified to in cases of spontaneous recovery following patients' falling in love.

Because the location of the heart chakra is at the center of the chakra system, its unsound functioning is manifested in egocentrism. The person is focused on him- or herself and does not relate to others or his or her surroundings. When this chakra is blocked and its activity is suppressed, the person is likewise blocked emotionally and is insensitive to others. This insensitivity can exist on various levels, all the way to total egoism, which is the exact opposite of love.

When the heart chakra is overactive, the person overidentifies with others, and can lose his or her center. A person who acts with excessive emotion is oversensitive and vulnerable; he or she draws in and absorbs others' emotions. Those who trigger such a person's compassion can—intentionally or not—drain his or her energy. The individual may also sacrifice him- or herself on the altar of others' needs, thereby sapping his or her reserves of energy until he or she is depleted of energy.

When Anahata is blocked, breathing is shallow, metabolism is slow, and the person may become phlegmatic and lacking vitality; his or her fonts of joy are likewise blocked. Deep breathing and focusing on the heartbeat are calming and encourage balanced functioning of this chakra. Concentrating on the color green also has a balancing effect and stimulates inner growth.

It is in the heart chakra that spiritual growth begins, and it develops the higher we move up in the chakra system. Meditating on this chakra enables us to experience joy, tranquility, and harmony, as well as love and openness toward others. It aids us in attracting people who are compatible with our energies, and strengthens our ability to give unconditional love, with the expectation of receiving nothing in return. Such love can only be given from the center of a person who is strong and confident, at peace with him- or herself, and who knows how to say no after opening the previous center, the power center. This person can also admit that he or she does not know it all, and is willing to open him- or herself up to absorbing knowledge, thereby preparing him- or herself for balanced functioning through the next chakra.

The fifth chakra, the **throat chakra**, or *Vishuddha*, is located in the area of the throat, and is connected to the thyroid gland. Its element is ether, and its main function is communication. The color associated with Vishuddha is light blue, a calming and quieting color that encourages creative and fluent communication. Vishuddha is depicted as a mandala in whose center is a triangle enclosing a circle, around which are sixteen petals. Numerologically, 16 is a number that expresses enmity and destruction, or spiritual wisdom. The same is true of words, the product of the throat chakra: words can hurt or soothe, destroy or praise. As the saying goes, "Life or death are in the power of the tongue." The throat chakra is ruled by Mercury, the planet representing communication in all its forms, and also by Neptune, the planet of spirituality and creativity, which is associated with the number 7, or the sum of 1 and 6, which form the number 16.

When this chakra functions soundly, all of the senses are sharpened; the person thinks clearly and speaks fluently and accurately. He or she uses various modes of expression and various channels. The individual states what he or she thinks, expresses his or her intentions clearly, and is heard correctly. The person does not let slip utterances that he or she regrets later on, and is not involved in gossip, nor does he or she chatter idly, a sign of overactivity of this chakra. On the other hand, the person remains silent when it is time to speak, a sign of underactivity.

A blockage in the throat chakra is formed when communication is cut off between a person and others, or when the person sharply judges or criticizes him- or herself or others. Wasted energy on insignificant relationships can cause a depletion of this chakra. The meaning of the word Vishuddha is "purification," and therefore meditation and work on this chakra enables undisrupted attention for the intake of messages from one's inner voice.

The **third eye chakra**, or *Ajna* chakra, is located slightly above the space between the eyebrows, and is associated with the pineal gland. (Some chakra systems associate the pineal gland with the crown chakra, and the pituitary gland with the third eye chakra.)

This chakra is also called the *eye of consciousness*; the meaning of the word Ajna is "to know." This chakra is depicted as a mandala with a triangle inside, around which are two petals symbolizing duality, or the separation between knowledge and the knower, the uniting of which can be achieved through meditation. The third eye chakra is associated with the number 6.

The color associated with this chakra is a bluish purple called indigo, which symbolizes intuition and spirituality. The development of this region enables intuitive knowledge, knowing the future, and seeing the hidden. This chakra's functions are imagination, dreaming, and telepathy.

When a person is not able to see things beyond his or her nose, or is limited to his or her physical senses—to the rational and the tangible—it means that this chakra is blocked. Such a person is not willing to accept what his or her eyes cannot see and what his or her brain does not comprehend. Some things are beyond conventional vision and reason, and through meditation on the third eye chakra, extrasensory vision can be developed and understanding of things beyond conventional vision can be achieved.

The **crown chakra**, the *Sahasrara*, or "thousand-petaled lotus," is located in the skull, and is associated with the pituitary gland. The color associated with Sahasrara is violet, which represents spirituality, and/or white, which reflects the entire spectrum. Opening this chakra brings about spiritual awakening. When we learn to concentrate on this chakra during meditation, we tune in to the higher self and to higher spiritual entities; we can receive an immediate solution to a problem, and insights regarding our path and our destiny are sharpened. The crown chakra is associated with the number 7.

In those who have achieved enlightenment, the crown chakra is quite developed, and indeed, the saints were depicted with halos in order to emphasize their higher spirituality. When we function through this chakra, we can tune in to total cosmic wisdom and experience unity with the infinite.

THE CHAKRAS AND THE PLANETS

The energy centers in the body are also associated with planets in our solar system. There are various ways to associate the planets with the chakras, and as this book deals with the planets from the karmic point of view, each of the seven *traditional planets* is associated with one of the seven chakras as follows:

- **Saturn** rules the root chakra; indeed, the beginning of our journey in life is represented by the Saturnian processes, which are connected to our karmic roots.

- **The Moon** rules the sacral chakra, and it represents our connection with the mother's womb. A balanced connection with the womb enables us to establish a sound sexual-emotional connection in our lives.

- **Mars**, the planet of action, rules the solar plexus chakra, which enables us to look out for our interests.

- **Venus**, the planet of love, rules the heart chakra, whose karmic purpose is unconditional love.

- **Mercury**, the planet of communication and mentality, rules the throat chakra.

- **Jupiter**, which is in charge of broad vision and spiritual growth, rules the third eye chakra.

- **The Sun**, the source of light and universal symbol of consciousness and knowledge, rules the crown chakra. Light is a source of information, and through the crown chakra we connect up with the ultimate light that is the source of infinite knowledge.

The *outer planets*, which are the higher octaves of the personal planets, also share in the control of our body's energy centers:

- **Pluto** is in charge of the first three chakras, the focus on which establishes the ego and assertiveness. Pluto teaches the proper use of power. It establishes physical power and survival in the root chakra; activates sexual and emotional power in the sacral chakra; and aids the development of willpower and the control of emotions in the solar plexus chakra. Through Pluto's action, inner conflicts are revealed. They rise to the surface, enabling their handling and resolution, which in turn is a necessary condition for spiritual development.

- **Neptune** embodies forgiveness, cosmic love, and spiritual vision and hearing, which in turn represent spiritual receptiveness as a whole. Neptune is in charge of the three middle chakras, which represent, respectively, emotion (heart), cognition (throat), and intuition (third eye), or the human functions that guide each of us.

- **Uranus**, in whose charge is supreme enlightenment, is associated with the crown chakra, through which insight is awakened, and through which a person's essence goes beyond his or her physical body and tangible reality.

From a karmic point of view, **Saturn** begins the karmic process, and **Uranus** completes it, so that Uranus represents the yearned-for release from the bonds of karma.

In the Age of Aquarius, the Age of Light and the domain of Uranus's responsibility, spiritual processes are more rapid, and we can experience "spiritual leaps." The Age of Aquarius is an era of change in thought patterns and lifestyles that brings about a raising of awareness. When work is done on the chakras, change can happen quickly; if the correct energetic work is done, personal liberation and the redemption of humanity are within reach.

DEVELOP YOUR ENERGETIC TOOLS

The vision of the redemption of humanity and of our planet can, in the New Age, become a reality. One of the paths to its realization is that each one of us works at developing the twelve centers of energy. When we work on the seven main chakras of the body, our focus is on the three-dimensional world. When we begin working on the chakras that extend beyond the body, we direct our consciousness to a four-dimensional reality or even beyond. We tune in to the reservoir of knowledge of the cosmic library, we gain access to our past lives and future lives, and we can become a channel of universal consciousness.

But first, we must perform the basic work with the seven centers of energy of the human body, as they serve as the foci of relating to ourselves, to others, to our surroundings, and to the universe. Work on the chakras must be done daily, as even a developed and balanced chakra can become closed for various periods or during certain events in our lives, or following contact with certain people.

Awareness and work on the chakras ensures constant balance, aids us in placing ourselves only in situations that are right for us to be in, and attracts to us those whose energies are compatible with our own, and to and from whom flows energy that enables a mutual "charging of batteries." The exercises offered herein are easy to do, and can be conveniently integrated into one's daily routine. They will help you maintain harmony, improve your existing relationship or help to attract a worthy and suitable partner, and help you reach and realize your potential in all dimensions—physical, mental, emotional, and spiritual. Above all, they will help you to tune in to your bliss sheath, to feel tranquility, joy, and eternal contentment.

Breathing in Light

The rhythm of our breathing is the rhythm of life; all exercises begin with breathing. The Hebrew words for "soul" *(neshama)* and "breath" *(neshima)* have the same root (נשׁם), as there is a connection between the two. We breathe as long as there is a soul within us, and breathing connects us to the soul. Conscious breathing connects us to our innermost levels and brings us into contact with the self, or our true essence.

When we breathe correctly, fully and without gasping, we are connected to ourselves with no blockages. Theoretically, if every minute of his or her life a person were to breathe perfectly and fully, his or her life would flow smoothly. But from life's first moment and throughout, for various reasons, blockages form and accumulate. These blockages are manifested in the way we breathe, and a reciprocal action forms: problems create blockages, and the resultant imperfect breathing creates more blockages. When we learn to breathe correctly, we begin to commune with the soul; when we retrain the entire organism to take in life energy, breathing takes us to the level of the soul.

Choose a period of time that you can count on to be free of disruptions, and find a pleasant place to sit. You can sit on the floor in a meditation position, or on a chair. If you choose a chair, place your feet flat on the floor.

Sit with your back straight and your eyes open. Begin breathing in the way you are used to, but be aware of the natural flow of your breathing. When the rhythm of your breathing is slow and relaxed, begin to be aware of your body parts one by one, beginning with your feet and moving up to your head. The awareness of each body part while continuing to breathe enables physical release and relaxation. When you are finished "traveling along" your body, inhale, hold your breath for a few seconds or for as long as it's comfortable, and exhale with a long "ahhhhhhhh." Repeat this exercise several times.

Continue breathing slowly and rhythmically. Direct your awareness to a ball of light twelve to twenty inches above your head. See or feel it glow and shine. Now, as you inhale, imagine that you connect with the ball, and draw the light inward with your inhalation. As you exhale, see or feel the light flowing through your body and exiting through the base of your body, i.e., your feet, if you are sitting on a chair, or your root chakra, if you are sitting on the floor.

With every inhalation that connects you with the ball of light above your head, you are aware of pure cosmic energy entering your body; with every exhalation, you admit light and let it flow through your body. You are aware that the light is washing away your fears and anxieties, tension and disquiet, and negative thoughts and feelings.

Be aware of the light also cleansing the negative karma that has accumulated in your consciousness in this life and over past incarnations.

Let this charged energy out of your body through its base and into the Earth. Continue thusly until you see or feel that the light leaving your body is as pure and clear as the light that you inhaled.

The grounding of the light into the Earth also serves to ground us. When we begin to commune with the spiritual heights, it is important to stay grounded to the Earth in order not to lose our connection with the physical world, the world in which we chose to function in this incarnation. Breathing in light connects us to both the heavens and to the Earth, uniting us with the entire cosmos.

Continue inhaling and exhaling; flow with your breathing for a few minutes. You are loose and relaxed, calm and tranquil. Now take a deep breath, and with it, connect up again to the ball of light above your head. A beam of light is going out of the ball and entering your crown chakra through an opening in your skull. You feel your crown chakra receiving the light, expanding and filling with light. Continue inhaling and exhaling until you sense that your crown chakra is filled with light.

Continue to inhale while connecting with the ball of light above your head. As you exhale, allow the light beam to enter your crown chakra through your skull, and this time continue down to your third eye chakra. Continue inhaling and exhaling, and being aware of your third eye chakra expanding. Continue inhaling and exhaling, and allow the third eye chakra to fill with light.

Continue inhaling and exhaling and connecting up to the ball of light. Allow the light beam to enter through the crown chakra down to the rest of the chakras in turn, and each time, fill them one by one with light: the throat, the heart, the solar plexus, the sacral, and the root. Continue inhaling and exhaling. All of your energy centers are open and glowing. Be aware of the light-filled chakras and of their pulsing with every inhalation and exhalation. The light not only illuminates but also awakens. It awakens all of the energy centers.

Sit thusly and continue with rhythmic breathing, and focus on the light-filled centers until you feel ready to finish. To exit the meditative state, begin to be aware of contact between your feet or hips and the Earth. Begin feeling your various body parts. Move your body gently. Blink your closed eyes gently, then open them. Tell yourself that you are alert and refreshed. Be aware of the light that has filled you even as you return to your everyday routine.

Coupling the Light Energies

To begin this exercise, repeat the first steps of breathing in light: Breathe slowly and rhythmically, relax all of your body parts, and be aware of the spontaneous flow of breathing for a few minutes. Now, as you inhale, connect up with the highest source of light that your consciousness has ever reached.

From this light source, a light beam emerges that comes down to your skull and washes the entire inside of your body. See or feel your entire body filled with light. Connect up again with the light source, and let the light beam wash the outside of your body. Be aware of the light washing all your bodies and cleaning all of your sheaths. Sit quietly, continue to inhale and exhale, and see your entire body glowing from within and from without.

It has already been said by sages that a person must purify his or her physical body until the divine light shines from within it, until the skin radiates light. (The Hebrew word for "light" [אור] and the Hebrew word for "skin" [עור] are pronounced the same ["OR"] even though they have different spellings.) After you have cleansed and purified yourself with the light, you are ready for work on couplehood.

If you wish to improve your present couple relationship, place an image of your partner opposite the place where you sit or stand (this exercise may be done standing), at a comfortable distance from yourself. If you want to attract a worthy and compatible partner, "place" an imaginary image facing you.

When you raise and heighten your energetic vibration, you direct yourself to partners who are on higher energetic levels. Exercising with the energy of the light will pull the right partner toward you naturally and effortlessly.

Perform a cleansing with light on the image of your real or imagined partner just as you cleansed yourself, until you see or feel him or her glowing from within and from without. Now take a deep breath and connect up to the ball of light above your head. As you exhale, draw in light through your crown chakra and move it to your heart chakra. See or feel your heart chakra fill with light. When it is full, the light begins to shift and flow toward the image of your partner, into his or her heart chakra.

See or feel the light enter your partner's heart chakra and expand the heart area until the entire chest cavity is filled with light. Lift the light up to his or her crown chakra, and from there, see it break out and move in an elliptical pattern toward your crown chakra (see figure 18). Let the light down into your heart chakra. Move the light back and forth in an elliptical pattern between you and your partner a few times, until you feel that an energetic connection has formed between you.

Allow yourself to experience an elevation of the spirit, the common linking to the light, the inner faith that everything will work out to everyone's satisfaction and that everything will unfold exactly as it should.

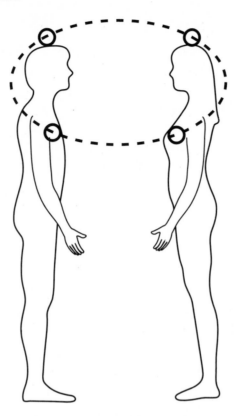

Figure 18—Attracting Your Soul Mate

Connecting Up to the Universal Energy

After relaxing all parts of your body, relax mentally as well by focusing on the natural flow of your breathing for a few minutes. Now breathe with awareness of each chakra. Focus on each of the chakras in turn, from lowest to highest. Breathe ten breaths for every chakra. Count only the inhalations; the exhalations will follow naturally.

Now, with as deep a breath as possible, connect up to the highest possible source of light. Think of cosmic consciousness, elevate yourself toward it, and connect up to the infinite source of light.

Notice that from this source of light a wide beam emanates. This beam opens all twelve of your energy centers and washes them with light. See the beam come down through the five energy centers above your head. See with your spirit's eye the highest center, the twelfth chakra, aligned in the heights of the universe. This twelfth chakra is filled with light that flows downward to the eleventh chakra.

See with your spirit eye this chakra located far, far above your head in the galaxy. The light fills it and comes down to the tenth chakra, which is high above your head in the solar system. See the light fill the tenth chakra.

Now the light shifts and comes down to the ninth chakra, which is several feet above your head. See or feel it filling with light. The ninth chakra is the chakra of Planet Earth; when you fill it with light, you attract the supreme light to our planet.

The light shifts and flows downward to the eighth chakra, which is twelve to twenty inches above your head. The light nears you, and you begin to feel the existence of the light. Your striving toward the light pulls it down to you; it enfolds you and bestows you its pure essence. See or feel the light fill the eighth chakra until it becomes a ball of light.

From there the light comes down to your crown chakra, which is open to receive it and absorb it. The chakra is full, and the light flows downward to all of the chakras beneath it. Experience each chakra glowing and sparkling.

Now redirect your consciousness to the high source of light. See and feel the light flow and come down to you. Let it fill you from within and enfold you from without. You are illuminated.

Experience your essence as pure Light.

You are existence that is all Light.

There is nothing but Light.

appendix a

THE DRAGON'S LOCATION

In the tables shown here, you can find the location of the Dragon's Head during the twentieth century. The Dragon's Tail is in the same degree, but in the opposing sign. For example:

If the Dragon's Head is at 19° Sagittarius, then the Dragon's Tail is at 19° Gemini.

PAIRS OF OPPOSITE SIGNS
Aries / Libra
Taurus / Scorpio
Gemini / Sagittarius
Cancer / Capricorn
Leo / Aquarius
Virgo / Pisces

THE LOCATION OF THE DRAGON'S HEAD
IN THE YEARS 1900–1950

01 / 01 1900 – 12 / 28 1900	Sagittarius
12 / 29 1900 – 07 / 17 1902	Scorpio
07 / 18 1902 – 02 / 04 1904	Libra
02 / 05 1904 – 08 / 23 1905	Virgo
08 / 24 1905 – 03 / 13 1907	Leo
03 / 14 1907 – 09 / 29 1908	Cancer

09/30 1908 – 04/18 1908	Gemini
04/19 1910 – 11/07 1911	Taurus
11/08 1911 – 05/26 1913	Aries
05/27 1913 – 12/13 1914	Pisces
12/14 1914 – 07/02 1916	Aquarius
07/03 1916 – 01/19 1918	Capricorn
01/20 1918 – 08/09 1919	Sagittarius
08/10 1919 – 02/26 1921	Scorpio
02/27 1921 – 09/15 1922	Libra
09/16 1922 – 04/04 1924	Virgo
04/05 1924 – 10/22 1925	Leo
10/23 1925 – 05/12 1927	Cancer
05/13 1927 – 11/28 1928	Gemini
11/29 1928 – 06/18 1930	Taurus
06/19 1930 – 01/06 1932	Aries
01/07 1932 – 07/25 1933	Pisces
07/26 1933 – 02/12 1935	Aquarius
02/13 1935 – 09/01 1936	Capricorn
09/02 1936 – 03/21 1938	Sagittarius
03/22 1938 – 10/09 1939	Scorpio
10/10 1939 – 04/27 1941	Libra
04/28 1941 – 11/15 1942	Virgo
11/16 1942 – 06/03 1944	Leo
06/04 1944 – 12/23 1945	Cancer
12/24 1945 – 07/11 1947	Gemini
07/12 1947 – 01/28 1949	Taurus
01/29 1949 – 08/17 1950	Aries

THE LOCATION OF THE DRAGON'S HEAD
IN THE YEARS 1950–2000

08/18 1950 – 03/07 1952	Pisces
03/08 1952 – 10/02 1953	Aquarius
10/03 1953 – 04/12 1955	Capricorn

04/13 1955 – 11/04 1956	Sagittarius
11/05 1956 – 05/21 1958	Scorpio
05/22 1958 – 12/08 1959	Libra
12/09 1959 – 07/03 1961	Virgo
07/04 1961 – 01/13 1963	Leo
01/14 1963 – 08/05 1964	Cancer
08/06 1964 – 02/21 1966	Gemini
02/22 1966 – 09/10 1967	Taurus
09/11 1967 – 04/03 1969	Aries
04/04 1969 – 10/15 1970	Pisces
10/16 1970 – 05/05 1972	Aquarius
05/06 1972 – 11/22 1973	Capricorn
11/23 1973 – 06/12 1975	Sagittarius
06/13 1975 – 12/29 1976	Scorpio
12/30 1976 – 07/19 1978	Libra
07/20 1978 – 02/05 1980	Virgo
02/06 1980 – 08/25 1981	Leo
08/26 1981 – 03/14 1983	Cancer
03/15 1983 – 10/01 1984	Gemini
10/02 1984 – 04/20 1986	Taurus
04/21 1986 – 11/08 1987	Aries
11/09 1987 – 05/28 1989	Pisces
05/29 1989 – 12/15 1990	Aquarius
12/16 1990 – 07/04 1992	Capricorn
07/05 1992 – 01/21 1994	Sagittarius
01/22 1994 – 08/11 1995	Scorpio
08/12 1995 – 02/27 1997	Libra
02/28 1997 – 09/17 1998	Virgo
09/18 1998 – 04/05 2000	Leo
04/06 2000 – 12/31 2000	Cancer

THE MAJOR ASPECTS

The planets lie at various distances from each other. These distances, or angular relation-ships between the planets, are formed by the geometric division of the 360° of the circle. They are measured in degrees and are called *aspects*.

There are *major aspects* and *minor aspects*. In this book we relate only to the major as-pects, which are:

Name of Aspect	Exact Aspect	Symbol
Conjunction	0°	☌
Sextile	60°	✶
Square	90°	☐
Trine	120°	△
Opposition	180°	☍

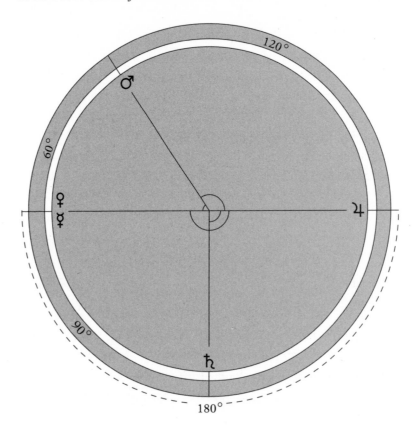

Figure 19—The Major Aspects

In figure 19:

- Venus and Mercury are in **conjunction**.
- Venus and Mercury **sextile** Mars.
- Venus and Mercury **square** Saturn.
- Mars is in **trine** to Jupiter.
- Jupiter is in **opposition** to Venus and Mercury.

The permitted orb of influence for the major aspects is 8°.

ORBS OF ASPECTS IN SYNASTRY

The orb of conjunction between planets that are placed in the same sign in two charts is 8°. The same applies to a conjunction between the planets and the nodes. When the planets involved in a conjunction are significant in the charts, the orb can be increased up to 10°.

In principle, the placement of significant planets in the same sign in both charts, even if the distance between them is greater, shows a tight connection between the two people. However, it is important to emphasize that the smaller the distance, the greater the effect; and an exact conjunction is the most effective of all.

Planets that are considered significant in synastry include the Sun, the Moon, the planets that rule the Sun and Moon signs, and the planets that rule the first and seventh houses in each chart, or planets located in these houses.

In addition, an orb of 2° is permitted when the planets are conjunct yet not in the same sign. For example, a planet in one chart that is placed at 29° Gemini, and a planet in a second chart placed at 1° Cancer, which immediately follows Gemini, are considered conjunct. (Such a conjunction is effective in a single chart, yet less so in a comparison chart).

When comparing charts for the purpose of determining karmic couplehood, we take into account all the major aspects (excluding the sextile, which is significant in a compatibility analysis, but less significant when we check karmic couplehood). The regular orb for the major aspects is 8°.

However, when significant planets are involved in an aspect, the orb can be increased up to 10°, yet as stated above, the smaller the orb, the more effective the aspect and the stronger and more significant the karmic relationship.

The orb of conjunction between planets and between the angular house cusps is 6°. The orb for the rest of the major aspects with the angular houses is 2°.

BIBLIOGRAPHY

Arroyo, Stephen. *Astrology, Karma & Transformation*. Davis, CA: CRCS Publications, 1987.

Carter, Charles E. O. *An Encyclopaedia of Psychological Astrology*. London: W. Foulsham & Co., 1926.

Devlin, Mary. *Astrology and Past Lives*. West Chester, PA: Para Research, 1987.

Donath, Emma Belle. *Have We Met Before?* Tempe, AZ: American Federation of Astrologers, 1982.

Greene, Liz. *Relating*. York Beach, ME: Samuel Weiser, 1978.

Hall, Judy. *The Karmic Journey*. London: Arkana, 1990.

Jung, C. G. *The Archetypes and the Collective Unconscious*. London: Routledge & Kegan Paul, 1959.

———. *Psychological Types*. London: Routledge & Kegan Paul, 1971.

Kaplan, Aryeh. *Jewish Meditation*. New York: Schocken Books, 1985.

Koparkar, Mohan. *Lunar Nodes*. New York: Mohan Enterprises, 1977.

Langley, Noel. *Edgar Cayce on Reincarnation*. New York: Warner Books, 1967.

Marciniak, Barbara. *Bringers of the Dawn*. Santa Fe, NM: Bear & Co., 1992.

Marks, Tracy. *Your Secret Self*. Sebastopol, CA: CRCS Publications, 1989.

Oken, Alan. *Alan Oken's Complete Astrology*. New York: Bantam Books, 1980.

Regush, Nicholas. *The Human Aura*. New York: Berkley, 1979.

Roberts, Jane. *The Seth Books*. New York: Bantam Books.

Sargent, Lois Haines. *How to Handle Your Human Relations.* Tempe, AZ: American Federation of Astrologers, 1958.

Schulman, Martin. *The Ascendant.* York Beach, ME: Samuel Weiser, 1988.

———. *Karmic Astrology.* York Beach, ME: Samuel Weiser, 1975.

———. *Karmic Relationships.* York Beach, ME: Samuel Weiser, 1984.

Sivananda, Swami. *Bliss Divine.* Sivanandanagar, India: Divine Life Society, 1974.

Stearn, Jess. *Intimates Through Time.* San Francisco, CA: Harper & Row, 1989.

———. *The Sleeping Prophet.* New York: Doubleday & Co., 1967.

Stone, Pauline. *Relationships, Astrology and Karma.* Wellingborough, UK: Aquarian Press, 1991.

Thornton, Penny. *Synastry.* Wellingborough, UK: Aquarian Press, 1982.

Vishnu-Devananda, Swami. *The Complete Illustrated Book of Yoga.* New York: Pocket Books, 1972.

———. *Meditation and Mantras.* New York: OM Lotus Publishing Co., 1978.

Woodroffe, John. *The Serpent Power.* Ganesh Press, 1973.

Zain, C. C. *The Next Life.* Los Angeles, CA: Church of Light, 1970.

A bibliography of books in Hebrew is available upon request from the author.